YOU CAN'T TAKE *New Orleans* OUT OF THE COOK

CHEF TOMMY CENTOLA
Creole Cajun Chef

living the life™

YOU CAN'T TAKE NEW ORLEANS
OUT OF THE COOK

LIVING THE LIFE published by
Ladero Press LLC
915 Doyle Road, Suite 303, Box #101
Deltona, Florida 32725

First Ladero Press Printing, November 2024

You Can't Take New Orleans Out of the Cook
Copyright © 2024 by Thomas Centola
All rights reserved.

ISBNs
978-1-946981-95-0 Hardback
978-1-946981-96-7 EPUB
978-1-946981-97-4 Kindle

Printed in the United States of America
Set in Times New Roman and Happy Memories
Cover Designed by SheerGenius
Edited by Zaundra George

All rights reserved. The reproduction, transmission, or utilization of this work in whole or in part in any form by any electronic, mechanical or other means, now known or hereafter invented, including xerography, photocopying and recording, or in any information storage or retrieval system, is forbidden without written permission.

For permission, please contact *Ladero Press Editors* at editors@laderopress.com.

The *Living the Life* logo is a trademark of Ladero Press.
The *Where Writers Can Soar* logo is a trademark of Ladero Press.

Library of Congress information available upon request.
www.laderopress.com

This book is dedicated to the two most important ladies in my life,
my mother and my wife.

Mom, I am glad that we shared a passion for food.
My only regret is that you are not here to see what I have accomplished.

Peggy, I don't know what I would do without you.
Thanks for everything you have given me.

I love you both.

TABLE OF CONTENTS

Introduction	14
New Orleans Traditions	17
Bananas Foster	18
Beignets	18
Blackened Redfish	19
Boiled Crawfish	20
Fried Seafood Po'boys	21
Jambalaya Cajun Style	21
King Cake	22
Muffuletta	23
Oysters Rockefeller	24
Pralines	25
Red Beans & Rice	25
Seafood Gumbo	26
Shrimp Remoulade	27
Appetizers	29
Artichoke Squares	30
Brie en Croûte	30
Cajun Fried Pickles	31
Cajun Hot Wings	31
Charbroiled Oysters	32
Crabmeat Ravigote	32
Crabmeat St. Francis	33
Crawfish Beignets	34
Crawfish Bread	34
Fried Artichoke Hearts	35
Fried Boudin Balls	35
Fried Crab Claws	36

- Fried Crawfish Tails 36
- Fried Eggplant Sticks 37
- Hot Crab Dip 37
- Hot Crawfish Dip 38
- Marinated Crab Claws 38
- Natchitoches Meat Pies 39
- Oysters Bienville 40
- Oysters Centola 41
- Oysters en Brochette 41
- Pomme Soufflé 42
- Seafood Crêpes 42
- Shrimp Rehoboth 43
- Spinach Dip 43
- Stuffed Artichokes 44
- Stuffed Mushrooms 45
- VooDoo Rolls 45

Soups 47
- Asparagus Soup 48
- Broccoli & Cheese Soup 48
- Chicken & Mushroom Soup 49
- Chicken and Sausage Gumbo 49
- Crab Bisque 50
- Crawfish Bisque 51
- Creole Onion Soup 51
- Gumbo Z'Herbs 52
- Oyster and Artichoke Soup 53
- Oysters Rockefeller Soup 54
- Oyster Soup 54
- Potato Soup 55
- Red Bean Soup 56
- Shrimp and Corn Chowder 56

Salads And Dressings 58
    Caesar Salad 59
    Cajun Popcorn Salad 59
    Fried Oyster Caesar Salad 59
    Godchaux Salad 60
    Muffuletta Salad 60
    Oriental Chicken Salad 61
    Perry Street Pasta Salad 62
    Uptown Salad 62
    Warm Spinach Salad 63
    1000 Island Dressing 63
    Bleu Cheese Dressing 64
    Caesar Dressing 64
    Honey Mustard Dressing 65
    Hot Bacon Dressing 65
    Thai Peanut Vinaigrette 65
    Vinaigrette Dressing 66

Seafood 67
    Alligator Sauce Picante 68
    BBQ Shrimp 68
    BBQ Shrimp & Grits 69
    Bronzed Grouper 70
    Catfish Étienne 70
    Catfish with Pecans 70
    Crab Cakes 71
    Crabmeat au Gratin 72
    Crawfish Étouffée 72
    Crawfish Pie 73
    Creole Catfish 74
    Fried Soft-Shell Crab with Crabmeat 74
    Frog Legs Abigail 75

Redfish Courtbouillon ... 76
Redfish Francis ... 76
Salmon Croquettes ... 77
Seafood Stuffed Mirliton ... 78
Shrimp Creole ... 78
Stuffed Crab ... 79
Stuffed Eggplant Pirogue Peggy ... 80
Stuffed Shrimp ... 81
Stuffed Trout ... 81

Meats ... 82

Boudin Stuffed Pork Chops ... 83
Bruccoloni ... 83
Bruno's Cajun Meatloaf ... 84
Cajun Fried Turkey ... 84
Chicken Bonne Femme ... 85
Chicken Cacciatore ... 86
Chicken Clemenceau ... 86
Chicken Delight ... 87
Chicken Florentine ... 87
Chicken Grande ... 88
Chicken Marsala ... 89
Chicken Oregano ... 89
Chicken Pontalba ... 90
Fried Chicken ... 90
Leg of Lamb ... 91
Osso Buco ... 92
Panéed Veal ... 93
Pork Chops and Artichoke ... 93
Turkey Poulet ... 94
Veal Andrew ... 94
Veal Marie ... 95

Veal Parmesan 95
Veal Piccata 96
Veal Saltimbocca 96

Pasta **98**

Chicken Pesto Pasta 99
Crabmeat Alfredeaux 99
Crawfish Fettuccini 100
Lasagna 100
Linguini with White Clam Sauce 101
Meatballs and Spaghetti 102
Oysters Bordelaise 102
Pasta Jambalaya 103
Shrimp and Tasso Pasta 103
Shrimp Fra Diavolo 104
Shrimp Pasta Lorraine 104
Shrimp Scampi 105

Sauces **106**

Alfredo Sauce 107
Béarnaise Sauce 107
Cream of Crawfish Sauce 107
Hickory Sauce 108
Hollandaise Sauce 108
Italian Red Sauce 109
Lemon Sauce 109
Meunière Sauce 109
New Orleans Bordelaise Sauce 110
Pesto 110
Roasted Garlic Crawfish Sauce 110
White Chocolate Sauce 111
White Sauce (Béchamel) 111

Side Dishes **112**

Brabant Potatoes	113
Cajun Boiled Potatoes	113
Carrots with Orange Glaze	113
Cinnamon Pecan Apples	114
Dirty Rice	114
Fried Okra	115
Fried Onion Rings	115
Fried Parsley	116
Garlic Mashed Potatoes	116
Hash Brown Potato Casserole	116
Herbed Rice Pilaf	117
Hurgy Lurgy	117
Hushpuppies	118
Maque Choux	118
Oyster Dressing	119
Sautéed Mushrooms and Onions	120
Sweet Potato Casserole	120
Vegetable Surprise	121

Desserts 122

Cheesecake	123
Chocolate Pecan Pie	123
Crème Brûlée	124
Crêpes Alyson	124
Fudge Brownie Pie	125
Fudge Pie	126
Lemon Ice Box Pie	126
Peanut Butter Ice Box Pie	127
Pecan Pie	127
Sour Cream Cake	128
Sweet Potato Pie	128
Turtle	129

White Chocolate Bread Pudding	130
White Chocolate Mousse	130

Brunch 132

How to Poach Eggs	133
Calas	133
Crawfish Omelet	134
Eggs Benedict	134
Eggs Pontchartrain	135
Eggs Sardou	135
Grillades and Grits	136
Oysters Benedict	137
Pain Perdu	137

Beverages 138

Absinthe Frappe	139
Simple Syrup	139
Bloody Mary	139
Brandy Milk Punch	139
Girl Scout Cookie	140
Hurricane	140
Irish Coffee	140
Mint Julep	141
Ramos Gin Fizz	141
Sazerac	141

Lagniappe 143

Blackening Seasoning	144
Bourbon Glaze	144
Cajun Popcorn Batter	144
Chicken Batter	145
Chicken and Pork Chop Marinade	145
Chicken Stock	146
Creole Seasoning Blend	146

Crêpe Batter 146

Egg Wash 147

Hawaiian Marinade 147

How to Make a Roux 147

Roasted Garlic 148

Seafood Breading 148

Seafood Seasoning Blend 148

Seafood Stock 149

About the Author 160

Acknowledgements

I wish to thank the following people:

My wife Peggy, for proofreading everything that I write
and for being the best wife a man could ask for.

My Mom & Dad ~ how I wish that they were here to see my accomplishments.

My siblings, Larry, Shelia, Ken, Lyle, Mike, Judy, and their families.
Your support means the world to me.

Bill Lottner for taking my cover photo.

My in-laws, Lorraine & Wesley, and their wonderful family.
Thanks for accepting me as your own.

And to all my friends, old and new, who have cheered me on throughout the years.

Introduction

Hurricane Katrina changed many people's lives. My change was a move to Arkansas. I think the biggest adjustment was the lack of Louisiana-type restaurants. When you live in a place all of your life, you do not realize that the food you are used to eating may not be available in other places. So, I took to my kitchen and started cooking all of the dishes that I missed so much from New Orleans: shrimp rémoulade, crab cakes, muffuletta, boiled crawfish, beignets, and king cake. The recipes that I have collected and created over the years are contained in these pages.

Growing up in New Orleans, I developed my love of food. That is probably not a surprise. New Orleans is a city in which, while at breakfast, we talk about what we are going to eat for lunch. At lunch, we talk about what we will have for dinner. At dinner, we discuss tomorrow's possibilities for dining. Most people eat to live; in New Orleans, we live to eat.

I was blessed with having the best teacher anyone could ask for: my mother, Mona. Growing up, I found myself spending time in the kitchen while she cooked. At eight years old, I was allowed to bake chocolate chip cookies by myself. The pride I felt as the cookies came out of the oven was unbelievable. I had actually created something, with my own hands that were being enjoyed by my family. I could not wait to try something else. Like my mother, I have acquired a large cookbook library. I often read cookbooks while eating lunch.

At sixteen, my first job was working at LeRuth's, a five-star restaurant in Gretna, Louisiana. Located across the river from New Orleans, LeRuth's was the best--in my opinion--restaurant in the city. While I was working as a busboy, I had access to a first-class kitchen. Watching the dishes being prepared was a great education. I saw the chefs work with ingredients I had never seen before: frog legs, lobster, veal, avocado, etc. I watched and asked questions. The chefs were happy to share their knowledge. With this knowledge, I started branching out at home. Veal Parmesan, stuffed shrimp, and turkey poulet were just a few of the new dishes I was cooking.

After working at other restaurants and retail stores, I became a manager at Cannon's Restaurant. Cannon's was located in the Oakwood shopping center in Gretna, Louisiana. My training started with me learning the kitchen. Working four months, learning every station, I soon became the kitchen manager. I enjoyed working with the cooks and jumping in when they needed my help. One day, the owner wanted me to work on a new project. The Sugar Busters diet, which began in New Orleans, was all everyone was talking about. I was asked to develop a sugar-free menu. On that menu was shrimp Alfredo with wheat pasta and fried oyster Caesar salad. The most popular dish I created for that menu was Creole catfish, a fried catfish fillet topped with a shrimp Creole sauce. I often miss the fun I had at Cannon's. The day I miss the most is the morning of Cleopatra's carnival parade. At 11:00 AM, most of the carnival organization would start their festivities. I would arrive at 8:00 AM and collect their preordered menus. I would then cook for the entire party while the employees got ready for the rest of the day. Just knowing that I could feed the all-female organization and start them on their way was just as pleasing as the day I first pulled those chocolate chip cookies out of the oven.

After Cannon's, I worked for Sysco Foods of New Orleans. Sysco is the largest food distributor in North America. At Sysco, I was able to increase my food knowledge. I was also able to help customers develop new menu items. It was a pleasure to work side by side with people trying to please the public with their food. Everything was good at Sysco until August 29, 2005.

We knew there was a hurricane brewing in the Gulf of Mexico. It was something I had lived with my whole life. Hurricanes came and went. You could leave town for a few days and return home to a false alarm. Only this time was different. Hurricane Katrina hit on August 29, 2005. We were in Shreveport, Louisiana, watching the news reports. I knew we were not going home in a few days. We decided to go to Arkansas, where my sister-in-law lived. When my wife, mother-in-law, and I arrived, we found that my other sister-in-law was already there. After two days, I was getting antsy. I called Sysco Foods of Arkansas to see if they had anything I could do to keep busy. I was told to come in the next day.

After about a month or so, my wife and I decided to stay in Arkansas. We bought a house and moved out of Gretna. At first, we enjoyed exploring our new surroundings; however, when we dined out, something was missing. The food was very different from what I grew up with. We even tried the local Cajun restaurant. It was good, but it seemed like the flavors were watered down. While I was able to get some items, fresh seafood was hard to find. Living in New Orleans, the availability of fresh seafood was right around the corner. Living in a new area, surrounded by land, made finding seafood difficult. Frequent trips to New Orleans allowed me to bring shrimp and crabmeat back to freeze. While shrimp and crabmeat froze well, the attempt to freeze oysters was a failure. The oysters lost the saltiness that made them delicious.

I finally found a Cajun seafood market fifteen minutes from my new home. They sold oysters by the pint. While they were not as good as shucking them yourself, they were a great substitute. I also found out that they boiled crawfish. I asked if they sold live crawfish; they said that they did. Also in their display cases, they sold andouille sausage, tasso, boudin, and frozen seafood--like redfish, grouper, crawfish tails, frog legs, crabmeat and shrimp. Now, it was time to start cooking the favorites with which I grew up.

When I first told people I was from New Orleans, they thought I was Cajun. What people outside of Louisiana do not realize is that most Cajuns live outside of the big cities. Not all of the food that comes from New Orleans is spicy and made with hot peppers. So, now, I take the time to explain to them about the cuisine of New Orleans. Yes, there are Cajun influences. I always felt my cooking was Creole with Cajun leanings. I come from an Italian family. Italian food is done differently in New Orleans. Creole Italian cooking comes from the Sicilians who came to New Orleans in the 1920s. They adapted their recipes to the local ingredients.

So, no New Orleans cookbook is complete without some Creole Italian dishes, which are included here.

I hope you enjoy these recipes as much as I have bringing them to you. I have a blog to promote these dishes and others that I am proud of: www.CreoleCajunchef.com. Be certain to visit and subscribe to receive our newsletter and recipes.

Here is a list of terms used in Louisiana cooking.

al denté – cooked so as not to be too soft: firm to the bite

Andouille Sausage is a spicy, heavily smoked pork sausage used in Creole and Cajun cooking.

Beignet is a New Orleans-style donut. It is square and served with powdered sugar on top.

Boudin is a sausage made with pork rice dressing.

Courtbouillon is a flavored liquid for poaching or quick-cooking foods.

Deglazing is to add a liquid to a pan in which meat has been roasted or sautéed, so that a sauce can be made that incorporates the cooking juices.

Étouffée literally means smothered. It does not have to contain a tomato-based sauce. I have examples of one with and one without tomato.

Filé is dried and ground leaves from the sassafras tree. It is used in Cajun cooking for thickening gumbos.

The Holy Trinity is the combination of onions, celery and bell peppers used as a seasoning base in Louisiana cooking.

Lagniappe means a little something extra given for free. A baker's dozen would be considered Lagniappe.

Mirlitons are also known as Chayote squash. Mirlitons are used quite a bit in South Louisiana cooking.

Roux is a cooked mixture of equal parts flour and fat (butter or vegetable oil). It is used as a thickening agent in many Creole and Cajun cooking.

Sauce Piquant is a tomato-based dish that can be a little on the spicy side.

Tasso is a spicy smoked pork shoulder. It is used to help season a dish.

New Orleans Traditions

To me, the following recipes represent the food that most people think of when they think of New Orleans. These are dishes that celebrate all that is New Orleans. They range from fancy oysters Rockefeller to the everyday fried seafood po'boy. In the 1980s, Cajun restaurants were popping up all over the country with blackened redfish as their signature dish. Every Mardi Gras season starts with a king cake party. Springtime brings crawfish, and no one needs an excuse for a crawfish boil. Red beans and rice every Monday. When it starts getting cooler, seafood gumbo warms your body and soul. Unique New Orleans dishes, muffuletta and jambalaya, are easily recreated. And for dessert, you can go simple: pralines and beignets, or flambéed bananas Foster. Any one of these dishes will have you longing for a walk along the Mississippi River.

Bananas Foster
Beignets
Blackened Redfish
Boiled Crawfish
Fried Seafood Po'boy
Jambalaya
King Cake
Muffuletta
Oysters Rockefeller
Pralines
Red Beans and Rice
Seafood Gumbo
Shrimp Remoulade

Bananas Foster

This wonderful dessert was created at Brennan's, one of the many famous restaurants in the city. New Orleans was the major port for bananas shipped from South America. Owen Brennan challenged his chef, Paul Blange, to create a dish including banana. The dish was named for a frequent customer and friend of Owen Brennan, Richard Foster. This dessert has become the most popular dish at Brennan's.

4 tablespoons butter, 1/2 stick
1 cup light brown sugar
1/2 teaspoon ground cinnamon
1/4 cup banana liqueur
4 bananas, cut in half lengthwise, then halved
1/4 cup dark rum
4 scoops of vanilla ice cream

Combine butter, sugar and cinnamon in a skillet. Place the pan over low heat and cook, stirring until the sugar dissolves. Stir in the banana liqueur, and then place bananas in the pan. When the banana sections soften and begin to brown, carefully add the rum. Continue to cook the sauce until the rum is hot, and then ignite the rum. When the flames subside, lift the bananas out of the pan and place 4 pieces over each portion of ice cream. Generously spoon warm sauce over the top of ice cream and serve immediately.

Beignets

To go to New Orleans and not eat beignets is like not going to New Orleans at all. Beignets are the New Orleans version of donuts. Café Du Monde is the most visited restaurant in town. Open twenty-four hours and only closed when Katrina came to town. Café Du Monde serves beignets as their only food. Beignets are delicious but can be dangerous. Often when you bite into one, you create a cloud of powdered sugar that goes everywhere. It is best not to wear dark clothes while eating beignets. When visiting New Orleans, make sure you do not miss out on this delightful experience!

1 1/2 cups lukewarm water
1/2 cup granulated sugar
1 envelope active dry yeast
2 eggs, slightly beaten
1 1/4 teaspoon salt
1 cup evaporated milk
7 cups bread flour, divided
1/4 cup shortening, softened
Peanut oil for frying
Powdered sugar

Mix water, sugar and yeast in a large bowl and let sit for 10 minutes. In another bowl, beat the eggs, salt and evaporated milk together. Mix the egg mixture into the yeast mixture. Add 3 cups of the flour to the mixture and stir to combine. Add the shortening and continue to stir while adding the remaining flour. Remove the dough from the bowl, place on a lightly floured surface and knead until smooth. Spray a large bowl with nonstick spray. Put the dough in the bowl and cover with a towel. Let the dough rise in a warm place for at least 2 hours.

Preheat peanut oil in a deep fryer to 350°F. Roll the dough out to about ¼-inch thickness and cut into 1-inch squares. Deep-fry, flipping constantly, until they become golden color. When beignets are done, quickly drain on paper towels, then sprinkle with powdered sugar. Serve immediately.

Blackened Redfish

This is the dish that started the Cajun food craze in America. Paul Prudhomme invented this dish when he opened his own restaurant. Having developed the opening menu for Mr. B's Bistro, he wanted to have a dish like their wood grilled redfish. Since he did not want to bring in a wood grill, he developed a blackening spice blend, coated a redfish fillet and cooked it in a very hot cast iron skillet. This dish became so popular around the country that a ban had been placed on fishing redfish. Now that the redfish population has become plentiful again, redfish is easier to find.

This dish is best cooked outdoors due to the smoke that the cooking process produces.

6 (8-ounce) redfish fillets
1 1/2 sticks of melted butter
Blackening Seasoning (page 144)

Heat a cast iron skillet over very high heat beyond smoking stage. You should see white ash in the skillet bottom in at least 10 minutes. The skillet cannot get too hot for this dish. Dip each fillet in the melted butter so that both sides are well-coated. Sprinkle a generous amount on the blackening seasoning evenly on both sides of the fillet, patting by hand. Place in the hot skillet and carefully pour 1 teaspoon of melted butter on top of each fillet (the butter may flame up). Cook uncovered over the same high heat until the underside looks charred, about 2 minutes (the time will vary according to the fillets' thickness and heat of the skillet). Turn the fish over and again pour 1 teaspoon of melted butter on top. Cook until fish is done, about 2 minutes more. Repeat with remaining fillets. Serve piping hot with melted butter in a small dish for dipping.

CHEF TOMMY CENTOLA

Boiled Crawfish

The best way to spend a Saturday afternoon is a crawfish boil with family and friends. It is one of the many things I have missed about moving from New Orleans. That is, until I was able to find live crawfish available locally. Now, I am able to share my love for crawfish with friends and family here in Arkansas. There is no limit to what you can include in a crawfish boil. Some of the non-traditional items you can boil are turkey necks, cauliflower, mushrooms and broccoli. I have even put some raw oysters in a small amount of the boiling water. They were nice and spicy.

Sack of crawfish (30 to 36 pounds), purged
2 boxes salt
1 (3-ounce) box Zatarain's Crab Boil in bag
1 pint Zatarain's Liquid Crab Boil
1 cup Zatarain's Dry Crab Boil
3/4 cup cayenne
6 large lemons, cut in half
6 yellow onions, peeled
6 heads garlic, peeled of outer skin but enough left to keep head in one piece
24 small new red potatoes
10 corn cobbettes
4 pounds smoked sausage, cut into bite size pieces

To Purge Crawfish
This is a very important step. This cleans the crawfish inside and out. Do not skip this step.

Pour live crawfish into an ice chest and sprinkle 1/2 box of salt on crawfish. Fill the ice chest with water until the crawfish are covered. Gently stir the crawfish to dilute the salt. Leave the crawfish in water for 10 minutes or so. This will cause the crawfish to purge themselves of mud and other things. Dump the water and purge one more time. After the second purge, rinse the crawfish until the water around them is clear.

To Cook Crawfish
Fill a large boiling pot* halfway with water (you can do two batches, if necessary). Begin heating water to a boil. When water begins to boil, add seasonings. After the water has been boiling for 5 minutes, add everything except crawfish. Boil for 10 minutes. Add crawfish and boil for 4 minutes. When done, turn off heat, cover the pot and allow to soak for 10 to 15 minutes. The longer you allow the crawfish to soak, the spicier they will become. Allow the crawfish to drain before dumping them on a newspaper-covered table. Let the feast begin!

* A boiling pot is a large pot with a strainer inside. They range in size from 22 to 80 quarts.

Fried Seafood Po'boys

Philadelphia has the hoagie. New England has the sub. A hot sub is also known as a grinder. In New Orleans, we have the po'boy. The po'boy sandwich was invented in the mid-1920s during a streetcar strike. Bennie and Clovis Martin served the striking workers sandwiches of roast beef gravy with bits of roast beef in the gravy on French bread for a nickel. When one would walk into the restaurant, workers would say, "Here comes one of those poor boys." New Orleanians would eventually shorten it to po'boys. After the strike, the sandwich became so popular that different variations of the sandwich started appearing. My favorite is the fried seafood po'boy. This can be made with any fried seafood: shrimp, oysters, catfish, soft-shell crab, etc.

Fried Seafood Po'boys (4 sandwiches)

2 pounds shrimp peeled, catfish, oysters or seafood of choice
Egg Wash (page 147)
Seafood Breading (page 148)
4 (8-inch) pieces of French bread, sliced in half lengthwise
Mayonnaise
Tomatoes sliced
Lettuce shredded
Pickle slices
Ketchup
Hot sauce (optional)

Heat a deep fryer to 350°F. Dip seafood in egg wash then coat with seafood breading. Shake off excess breading before putting in the fryer. Cook until seafood starts to float. Drain on a paper towel lined plate. Prepare bread with mayonnaise, tomato, lettuce, pickles, ketchup, and hot sauce. Add seafood and serve immediately.

Jambalaya Cajun Style

This dish was an attempt to recreate Spanish paella while New Orleans was under Spanish rule. Jambalaya, like gumbo, was made with whatever the cook had left over from previous meals. This is one of my favorite meals and one of the first I learned to cook. What makes this a Cajun dish as opposed to a Creole dish is the absence of tomato. Tomatoes are not used in Cajun cooking. I have added a step at the bottom to make this a Creole jambalaya.

1 pound andouille sausage, cut into bite size pieces
1 cup chicken meat, cut into bite size pieces
1/3 cup onion, chopped

1/4 cup celery, chopped
1/4 cup green bell pepper, chopped
1/4 cup garlic, minced
2 tablespoons olive oil
1 quart beef stock
1 quart *Chicken Stock* (page 146)
2 tablespoons salt
2 tablespoons basil
2 tablespoons oregano
2 tablespoons *Creole Seasoning Blend* (page 146)
1 tablespoon paprika
2 cups long grain rice

Over medium heat, cook sausage, chicken, onions, celery, bell pepper, and garlic in olive oil. Add stock and dry seasonings. Bring to a boil. Add rice. Cover and lower heat to low. Cook until all of the liquid is absorbed, about 20-25 minutes. To make this jambalaya a Creole jambalaya, add a small can of tomato sauce with the stock.

King Cake

King cake is a type of pastry associated with Mardi Gras season. The season starts on January 6th, the twelfth day of Christmas and continues until Mardi Gras day. The cake has a small trinket (often a small plastic baby, sometimes said to represent Baby Jesus) inside. In earlier times, carnival organizations used the king cake to select their royalty for their coming year's festivities. Most people have weekly king cake parties. The person finding the trinket is responsible for throwing the next party and supplying the king cake.

Cake
1 tablespoon light brown sugar, packed
1 tablespoon cinnamon
1/2 cup warm water
1 package active dry yeast
3/4 cup warm milk
4 cups all-purpose flour
1 large egg, slightly beaten
1/4 cup granulated sugar
2 tablespoons canola oil
1 teaspoon salt

Preheat oven to 400°F. Spray a 13x9 inch-baking pan with non-stick cooking spray. In a small bowl, combine brown sugar and cinnamon; set aside. Combine the warm water and yeast in a large mixing bowl and let stand until the yeast is dissolved, about 5 minutes. Stir the warm milk into the yeast mixture. Add 1 cup of flour, eggs, sugar, oil, and salt until well blended. Add remaining flour, 1/2 cup at a time, until the dough becomes very stiff. Turn dough on to a lightly floured surface and knead until smooth and elastic, about 10 minutes. Roll the dough out into a 12x8 oval. Sprinkle evenly with the brown sugar-cinnamon mixture. Cover with a towel and let rise in a warm place until doubled in volume, about 1 hour. Bake 12-15 minutes or until browned. Invert pan onto a platter and let cool.

Decorations for Top of Cake
1/2 cup powdered sugar
1 tablespoon cream cheese
1 teaspoon vanilla extract
1 tablespoon water
Purple, green and gold colored sugar

In a small bowl, combine the powdered sugar, cream cheese, vanilla, and water. Stir until creamy and spread evenly over the warm cake. Alternating colors, sprinkle purple, green and gold sugars over cake.

Muffuletta

This sandwich is a unique New Orleans creation. The Central Grocery, in the French Quarter, is credited with its invention, according to the following story:

Most of the farmers in the French Market were Sicilian. They used to go to Central Grocery for lunch. They would order some salami, ham, a piece of cheese, a little olive salad and some bread. They would then proceed to eat them separately. The owner of Central Grocery suggested that they cut the bread and put everything inside and eat it like a sandwich. Muffuletta bread, a round Sicilian sesame bread, was softer that an Italian twist loaf, so it was used to make the sandwich. The other main ingredient is the olive salad. This is a mixture of olives, garlic, capers, seasonings, and olive oil. This is made in advance and tastes better after sitting a day. The sandwich is usually too large for a single portion. Most places sell it in half and quarters.

1 muffuletta bread or loaf of French bread
Olive salad, recipe to follow
Olive oil
6 ounces Genoa salami, thinly sliced
6 ounces ham, thinly sliced
5 ounces provolone cheese, thinly sliced
5 ounces mozzarella cheese, thinly sliced

Olive Salad

2/3 cup large green olives, pitted and coarsely chopped
2/3 cup medium green olives, pitted and coarsely chopped
1 (16oz) jar giardiniera
1/2 cup pimentos, chopped
4 cloves garlic, minced
1 tablespoon capers, drained and rinsed
1/2 cup fresh parsley, finely chopped
1 teaspoon fresh oregano, finely chopped
1 tablespoon red wine vinegar
3/4 cup extra-virgin olive oil

In a medium bowl, combine all ingredients and then allow the flavors to blend for at least 2 hours prior to serving. Store, covered, in the refrigerator until ready to use.

Sandwich

Slice bread in half crosswise. Brush the bottom of the loaf with juice from the olive salad. Layer salami, ham, provolone, and mozzarella on the bottom half. Top with as much olive salad as will fit without spilling over the side. Add bottom side and press down slightly. Serve at room temperature. Some people like them toasted. To toast, put both sandwich halves in an oven preheated to 350 degrees for a few minutes.

Oysters Rockefeller

This rich oyster dish was created at Antoine's restaurant, New Orleans's oldest restaurant. In 1899, Jules Alciatore, the son of founder Antoine Alciatore, was looking for a locally available ingredient to replace French snails, which was in short supply. Using ingredients that were left over from other dishes, Jules found his substitute. The original recipe has never left the kitchen at Antoine's. Most recipes contain spinach, which is one ingredient that the family says is not in the dish. So, here is my interpretation.

4 sprigs flat-leaf parsley
4 green onions, green and white parts
1/2 cup fresh celery leaves
8 fresh tarragon leaves
8 fresh chervil leaves
1/2 plain breadcrumbs
1 1/2 sticks (12 tablespoons) butter, soften
1 teaspoon *Creole Seasoning Blend* (page 146)
1/4 teaspoon hot sauce
24 oysters, freshly shucked, on the half shell; oyster liquid reserved

Rock salt

Mince together parsley, green onions, celery leaves, tarragon, and chervil as finely as you can. If you think you have minced them enough, mince them some more. Mix together with the breadcrumbs and butter to make a smooth paste. Mix in Creole seasoning and hot sauce. Preheat your broiler. Lower the top rack to the middle of the oven. Spread rock salt over a large baking sheet pan, this will keep the oysters from moving. Place the shells in the salt, making sure they are level. Place an oyster in each shell, plus a little bit of the oyster liquor. Spoon an equal amount of the herb mixture over each oyster. Place the pan on the middle rack and broil until the oysters have curled and the sauce is bubbling, about 5 minutes. Keep an eye on them; you don't want to overcook them. Serve immediately.

Pralines

In France and everywhere else, praline is a generic term for any candy made with nuts. In New Orleans, pralines are candy made with Louisiana pecans and cream. Throughout the French Quarter, pralines can be seen made in open kitchens in some shops. They are the perfect souvenirs to bring home from New Orleans. The good thing is that they are easy to make at home.

2/3 cup sugar
2/3 cup light brown sugar
1/2 cup evaporated milk
3 tablespoons vanilla extract
1/2 stick (4 tablespoons) of butter, cut into 1-tablespoon pieces
1 cup chopped pecan pieces

Add both sugars and milk in a saucepan over medium high heat. Heat and stir about 15 to 18 minutes, to a softball stage.* Cook 3-4 minutes longer. Take off heat. Add butter and vanilla. Let the butter melt then add pecans slowly and mix well. Spoon on wax paper to cool.

* A softball stage is 235-240 degrees. At this temperature, the sugar mixture dropped into cold water will form a soft, flexible ball. If you remove the ball from the water, it will flatten as you roll it between your fingers.

Red Beans & Rice

In New Orleans, red beans and rice are traditionally served on Mondays. In earlier times, Monday was washday. A pot of red beans could sit on the stove and simmer for hours while women were busy scrubbing clothes. Many restaurants still serve this as a Monday special. Red beans and rice were the favorite food of

Louis Armstrong, the famous New Orleanian trumpeter. He would sign his name *Red Beans and Ricely Yours, Louis Armstrong.*

1 pound dried red beans, preferably Cameilla Brand, rinsed and sorted over
3 tablespoons vegetable oil
1/4 cup chopped tasso
1 1/2 cups onions, minced
3/4 cup celery, minced
1/2 teaspoon salt
1/2 teaspoon ground black pepper
2 bay leaves
2 tablespoons fresh parsley, chopped
1 tablespoon dried thyme
1 1/2 pounds smoked sausage or andouille, cut into 1-inch pieces
3 tablespoons garlic, chopped
10 cups *Chicken Stock* (page 146)
4 cups cooked white rice

Place the beans in a large bowl or pot and cover with water plus 2 extra inches. Let soak for at least 8 hours. Drain and set aside. In a large pot, heat vegetable oil over medium-high heat. Add the tasso and cook, stirring, for 1 minute. Add onions and celery to the pot. Season with salt and pepper, and cook, stirring, until the vegetables are soft, about 4 minutes. Add bay leaves, parsley, thyme, and sausage, and cook, stirring, to brown the sausage, about 4 minutes. Add the garlic and cook for 1 minute. Add beans and stock, stir well, and bring to a boil. Reduce the heat to medium low and simmer, uncovered, stirring occasionally, until the beans are tender and start to thicken, about two hours. Should the beans become too thick and dry, add more stock, about 1/4 cup at a time. Remove from heat and with the back of a heavy spoon, mash about 1/4 of the beans against the side of the pot. Continue to cook until the beans are tender and creamy, 15-20 minutes, removing bay leaves. Serve over rice.

Seafood Gumbo

Gumbo is a dish that has many variations. This dish, like jambalaya, can be made with whatever meats or seafood you have on hand. But to me, gumbo means *seafood* gumbo. This wonderful soup is served in almost every restaurant in New Orleans. While you can use different seafood, most gumbos are thickened with okra or filé, which I prefer. Filé is ground sassafras leaves.

3/4 cup vegetable oil
3/4 cup flour
2 cups onion, chopped
1 cup green bell peppers, chopped

1 cup celery, chopped
2 tablespoon garlic, chopped
1 tablespoon salt
1/2 teaspoon black pepper
1/2 teaspoon cayenne pepper
5 bay leaves
8 cups *Seafood Stock* (page 149)
6 jumbo crabs, broken in half
1 pound medium shrimp, peeled and deveined
1 pound crabmeat (lump or claw)
2 dozen shucked oysters
1/4 cup green onions, chopped
1/4 cup fresh parsley, chopped
Cooked rice
Filé powder

Combine oil and flour in a large cast-iron pot over medium heat. Stirring slowly and consistently for 20 to 25 minutes, making a dark roux, the color of chocolate. Add onions, bell pepper, celery, garlic, salt, black pepper, cayenne and bay leaves. Cook, stirring occasionally, for about 10 minutes, or until vegetables are soft. Set heat to low. Add shrimp stock or water; stir to blend. Add crab and simmer, uncovered, stirring occasionally for 1 1/2 hours. Add the shrimp and crabmeat and cook for 15 minutes. Add oysters, green onions and parsley; cook 2 to 3 minutes, or until the edges of the oysters curl. Remove from heat. Remove bay leaves. Serve over rice and pass the filé powder at the table.

Shrimp Remoulade

Of all of the traditional recipes from New Orleans, this one is the most special to me. This shrimp remoulade recipe is the one that my mother Mona served. It would not be a Christmas dinner without shrimp remoulade. I hope it brings good memories to you. Most remoulade sauces you find contain mayonnaise. This one does not. When I lived in New Orleans, the horseradish mustard was a hard ingredient to find. On one of my first trips to a grocery store in Arkansas, I found three different brands. I understand it is making a comeback in New Orleans.

4 tablespoons horseradish mustard
1/2 cup tarragon vinegar
1/2 teaspoon cayenne pepper
2 tablespoons ketchup
1 clove garlic, crushed
1 teaspoon salt
1 tablespoon paprika

CHEF TOMMY CENTOLA

1 cup salad oil
1/2 cup celery, diced
1/2 cup green onion, diced
2 pounds shrimp, medium size, boiled & peeled

Mix mustard, vinegar, cayenne pepper, ketchup, garlic, salt, and paprika. Add oil, beating well. Add celery and green onions. Add shrimp and refrigerate for at least 2 hours. Serve on shredded lettuce.

Appetizers

The definition of an appetizer is a small portion of food served before or at the beginning of a meal to stimulate the desire to eat. While this is true, I think that appetizers can be a meal in themselves. When my family gets together to open Christmas presents, everyone brings appetizers so we do not have to take time to sit down to eat. Everyone can eat at their own pace without stopping the party. On most Chinese restaurant menus, there is a large platter with several appetizers on them. One person could make a meal out of one platter. There are restaurants where you can make your own appetizer platter from the menu. A great appetizer takes as much talent to make as a great entrée. Cook up a couple one night for dinner. You will be glad you did.

Artichoke Squares 30
Brie en Croûte 31
Cajun Fried Pickles 32
Cajun Hot Wings 33
Charbroiled Oysters 34
Crabmeat Ravigote 35
Crabmeat St. Francis 36
Crawfish Beignets 38
Crawfish Bread 39
Fried Artichoke Hearts 40
Fried Boudin Balls 41
Fried Crab Claws 42
Fried Crawfish Tails 43
Fried Eggplant Sticks 44

Hot Crab Dip 45
Hot Crawfish Dip 46
Marinated Crab Claws 47
Natchitoches Meat Pies 48
Oysters Bienville 49
Oysters Centola 50
Oysters en Brochette 52
Pomme Soufflé 53
Seafood Crêpe 54
Shrimp Rehoboth 55
Spinach Dip 56
Stuffed Artichoke 57
Stuffed Mushrooms 58
Voodoo Rolls 59

Artichoke Squares

Artichokes were one of my mother's favorite ingredients. She used them in every course except desserts. Here is one of her appetizers. It is an easy dish to make. This dish needs to be refrigerated before serving which makes it a perfect dish to serve while cooking others.

1 can artichoke hearts
1 cup Italian bread crumbs
1/2 cup Parmesan cheese, grated
1/2 cup olive oil
2 cloves garlic, minced
1 egg

Preheat oven to 350°F.

Drain artichoke hearts and set juice aside in a bowl. Mash hearts and add breadcrumbs, cheese, olive oil, and garlic. Add egg to reserved juice and beat. Pour mixture into a buttered 8x8 casserole dish. Bake in oven for 30 minutes. Let cool, then refrigerate. Cut into squares before serving.

Brie en Croûte

This dish is in memory of my sister-in-law Denny. Whenever our family got together, quite often everyone brought an appetizer for snacking. Denny often brought this delicious treat. She had a smile that lit up the room. She is sorely missed but remembered lovingly.

1 sheet frozen puff pastry
1 egg, slightly beaten
1 tablespoon water
1/4 cup toasted pecan pieces
1/4 cup fresh parsley, chopped
1 pound brie cheese round

Thaw pastry sheet at room temperature for 30 minutes. Preheat oven to 400°F. Mix egg and water. Unfold pastry sheet on a lightly floured surface. Roll into 14-inch square. Cut off the corners to make a circle. Sprinkle pecans and parsley in the center of the pastry. Top with the brie. Brush the edge of the pastry circle with egg mixture. Fold two opposite sides over brie. Trim the remaining two sides to 2 inches from the edge of the brie. Fold these two sides onto the brie. Press edges to seal. Place seam-side down on a baking sheet. Decorate the top with pastry scrapes if desired. Brush with egg mixture. Bake 20 minutes or until golden brown. Let stand 1 hour. Serve with crackers.

Cajun Fried Pickles

It seems like they will deep-fry anything at the Arkansas State Fair. While fried pickles are not new here, I have never heard of Cajun fried pickles. When a friend asked me on my blog if I had a recipe for them, I figured it was time to make one. I prefer to use pickle slices instead of spears. You get a more uniform fry on the slices.

Dill pickle slices
1 egg, beaten
1 cup milk
1 tablespoon Worcestershire sauce
6 drops hot sauce
2 cups + 1 tablespoon flour
1 tablespoon *Creole Seasoning Blend* (page 146)

Heat fryer to 350°F.

Mix egg, milk, Worcestershire, hot sauce, and 1 tablespoon flour in a bowl. Mix 2 cups flour and Creole seasoning to taste in a bowl. Double batter pickles by dipping in milk mixture then flour and repeat. Fry pickles until golden brown.

Cajun Hot Wings

This is not a recipe for buffalo wings. Cajuns use all of the available food to nourish their bodies. So instead of chicken wings, I am using frog legs. Frogs are plentiful in the swamps of Louisiana. People say that frog legs taste like chicken. What do you think?

9 pair frog legs
Egg Wash (page 147)
Seafood Breading (page 148)

Sauce
6 tablespoons butter
1/4 cup hot sauce
1 teaspoon granulated garlic

Preheat a deep fryer to 350°F. Separate frog legs and dip in egg wash. Coat frog legs in seafood breading. Shake off excess breading and place in deep fryer. Fry in two or more batches to avoid overcrowding. When they are golden brown, remove from fryer and drain on paper towels. Place in a medium bowl. Melt butter over medium heat. Add hot sauce and garlic; cook for 2 minutes. Pour sauce on top and toss to coat. You can adjust the heat of this dish by adding or subtracting hot sauce to taste.

Charbroiled Oysters

This dish is the best new oyster dish to come out of New Orleans in many years. The dish originated at Drago's restaurant in Metairie, a suburb of New Orleans. It is so popular and has shown up on many menus in the New Orleans area. It is a great dish when entertaining outside. Just be careful, they are addictive.

2 sticks butter, softened
3 tablespoons garlic, chopped
3/4 teaspoon ground black pepper
1/2 teaspoon Italian seasoning
1 1/2 dozen oysters on the half shell
1/4 cup Parmesan cheese, grated
2 1/2 teaspoons fresh parsley, chopped

Mix butter, garlic, pepper, and Italian seasonings together in a bowl. Heat a grill, either gas or charcoal, and put the oysters still in their shell over the hottest part of the grill. Spoon enough of the seasoned butter over the oysters so that some of it will overflow into the fire and flame up a bit. The oysters are ready when they puff and get curly on the edges. Sprinkle the Parmesan cheese and parsley on top. Serve on the shell immediately with hot French bread to soak up the sauce.

Crabmeat Ravigote

This dish, along with shrimp remoulade, are the two most popular cold appetizers in New Orleans. These dishes were originally created to take crabmeat that was close to going bad and make it taste good. The word ravigote means revived. Someone wondered how would this dish taste using fresh crabmeat. Of course, the dish tasted 100% better.

2 teaspoons garlic, minced
2 tablespoons fresh parsley, chopped
6 tablespoons red onion, minced
2 tablespoons capers, chopped
1 teaspoon *Seafood Seasoning Blend* (page 148)
2 tablespoons lemon juice
1 pound lump crabmeat, cleaned of shells
1/4 cup Creole mustard
1/4 cup mayonnaise
1 teaspoon prepared horseradish
12 thick tomato slices
Shredded lettuce

In a mixing bowl, combine garlic, parsley, onions, capers, seafood seasoning, and lemon juice. With a fork, mash and stir the ingredients in the bottom of the bowl to allow the flavors to blossom. Let sit for 2 minutes. Add crabmeat, mustard, mayonnaise, and horseradish. Toss gently but thoroughly. Refrigerate for at least 1 hour. Top four small plates with shredded lettuce. Place three tomato slices in a circle on each plate. Top with 1/4 of the crabmeat mixture.

Crabmeat St. Francis

My first job at LeRuth's restaurant featured this dish. I had lots of fun while watching chefs Warren, Larry and Lee Leruth make their magic. This recipe was their most popular dish. Never have I tasted a dish as good as this.

3 tablespoons butter
1 small green onion, finely chopped
1 large clove garlic, finely chopped
3/8 cup yellow onions, finely chopped
3/8 cup celery hearts, finely chopped
1 sprig fresh thyme, finely chopped
1/2 teaspoon salt
Pinch of celery seed
1/8 teaspoon cayenne pepper
1/8 teaspoon white pepper
1/8 teaspoon black pepper
2 bay leaves
3/8 cup flour
1 pint heavy cream, gently boiling
1 cup *Seafood Stock* (page 149), gently boiling
1/8 cup Chablis wine
1 tablespoon fresh parsley, chopped
2 egg yolks
1 pound jumbo lump crabmeat, picked over for shell pieces
Seasoned bread crumbs
6 tablespoons melted butter
6 casserole dishes

In a deep sauté pan, heat the butter. Add green onion, garlic, onion, celery heart, and all spices. Stir in flour and make a vegetable roux, stirring continuously. Allow to cook over low heat for 5 minutes. Add boiling cream, seafood stock and wine. Bring to a boil. Reduce and simmer 15 minutes, then add parsley. On low heat, stir in the yolks. Remove from direct heat and stir well.

Keep warm. Preheat oven to 400°F. Divide the crabmeat into the casserole dishes. Cover with approximately 1/2 cup of sauce and bake until bubbly and browned, about 12-15 minutes. Sprinkle breadcrumbs on top and spoon 1 tablespoon melted butter over each dish. Serve immediately.

Crawfish Beignets

This dish combines the wonderful beignet with fresh boiled crawfish. Beignets are very versatile. They are great for breakfast with powdered sugar. They take on a different mealtime when you add seafood to the mixture. Crawfish beignets are great when dipped into Creole mustard.

2 eggs
6 ounces crawfish tails, cleaned
1 teaspoon *Seafood Seasoning Blend* (page 148)
1/4 cup green bell pepper, finely chopped
1/4 cup green onion, finely chopped
1 tablespoon garlic, minced
1 teaspoon baking powder
1 1/2 cups flour
1/2 cup milk
Creole Seasoning Blend (page 146)

Heat deep fryer to 365°F. Mix eggs in a large bowl until foamy. Add crawfish to the eggs in the bowl. Sprinkle with seafood seasoning. Stir in bell pepper, green onion, garlic, baking powder, flour, and milk with the egg mixture. This should be stirred to a thick consistency. Drop 1 tablespoon of the mixture into fryer, one at a time, not crowding the oil. Let them fry for about 3 minutes, turning to ensure browning on both sides. Remove the beignets and drain on paper towels. Sprinkle with Creole seasoning while hot.

Crawfish Bread

Crawfish Bread can be done two ways. Most people make a crawfish mixture and spread it on French bread. My recipe is a little bit different. My crawfish bread is made like a loaf of bread with crawfish and seasonings mixed in the dough. It is a little different but very tasty.

1/2 cup butter, melted
2 cups all-purpose flour, sifted
3 large eggs
1 teaspoon salt
1 1/2 teaspoon baking powder
1 cup milk
1 teaspoon fresh thyme, chopped

1/4 cup green onion, chopped
1/4 cup fresh parsley, chopped
10 ounces crawfish tails, roughly chopped

Preheat oven to 375°F.

Oil and flour a 9x13x2-inch baking pan. In a mixing bowl, mix butter, flour and eggs, making a smooth mixture with no lumps. Add the remaining ingredients and combine. Pour batter into prepared pan and bake for 30 to 40 minutes until done.

Fried Artichoke Hearts

Artichokes are prominent in Creole Italian cooking. The crunch of the bread crumbs contrasts with the soft artichoke hearts. It is a great way to start your meal. Combine these with boudin balls and eggplant sticks and you have a great combination platter.

3 cups flour
2 tablespoons *Creole Seasoning Blend* (page 146)
36 quartered pieces artichoke hearts
3 cups seasoned bread crumbs
Chicken Batter (page 145)

Heat deep fryer to 350°F. Mix Creole seasoning with flour. Roll hearts in flour; dip them into the chicken batter; roll them in the breadcrumbs shaking off the excess. Fry them until they are golden brown and floating. Serve them with ranch dressing.

Fried Boudin Balls

Boudin is a sausage made from pork rice dressing. Cajuns make boudin in many different varieties. I am particularly fond of crawfish boudin. You can find regular boudin in the sausage section of grocery stores. Boudin balls are a delicious start to a crawfish boil.

2 cups corn flour
1/8 teaspoon dried thyme
1/8 teaspoon dried basil
1/8 teaspoon dried marjoram
Creole Seasoning Blend (page 146)
1 package boudin
Canola oil for frying

Preheat deep fryer to 375°F.

Season corn flour with thyme, basil, marjoram, and Creole seasoning. Cut the boudin into 2-inch pieces and roll them in a ball. Roll in corn flour, shaking off the excess. Fry for 3-4 minutes, or until golden brown. Serve hot.

Fried Crab Claws

I love the blue crab available in Louisiana. To me, they have the best flavor of all species of crab. Fried crab claws are a delightful way to start off a meal. They cook up very quickly. You can fry them up at the last minute, so you can spend your time preparing other dishes.

1 pound peeled crab claws
Egg Wash (page 147)
2 cups *Seafood Breading* (page 148)

Heat a deep fryer to 375°F.

Dip crab claws in egg wash. Allow them to drain, and then dredge them in the breading. Shake off the excess breading and fry them for 2-3 minutes, or until golden brown. Serve them with cocktail sauce or remoulade sauce.

Quick Cocktail Sauce Recipe

Ketchup
Prepared horseradish
Lemon juice

Mix desired amounts of the above ingredients in a small bowl until well combined.

Fried Crawfish Tails

Fried crawfish tails have been around for a long time. When Paul Prudhomme started calling them Cajun popcorn, they had a rebirth. You can find these in most Cajun restaurants when crawfish are in season (springtime). Any crawfish found other times are going to be frozen crawfish.

2 cups corn flour
1 tablespoon salt
1 tablespoon black pepper
1 tablespoon paprika

1 pound crawfish tails peeled
Egg Wash (page 147)

Preheat deep fryer to 350°F. Mix corn flour with salt, pepper and paprika. Dip the crawfish in the egg wash. Allow them to drain, and then dredge them in the corn flour mixture. Fry for 2-3 minutes or until golden brown. Serve with hollandaise sauce or remoulade sauce.

Fried Eggplant Sticks

This appetizer was one of the popular appetizers at Cannon's restaurant. They can be prepared in advance so that all you have to do is drop them in the fryer. But do not make them too far in advance; the breadcrumbs can become soggy. If they do, just re-bread them with breadcrumbs. They are best served with hollandaise sauce.

3 eggplants, peeled and cut into ½ inch strips
1 cup flour
Chicken Batter (page 145)
2 cups Italian bread crumbs
Grated Parmesan cheese

Heat deep fryer to 350°F. Cover eggplant sticks with flour, shaking off the excess. Dip the sticks into batter. Remove and shake off the excess. Roll sticks in breadcrumbs until fully covered. Fry for 2-4 minutes or until golden brown. Drain on paper towels, and sprinkle with Parmesan cheese before serving.

Hot Crab Dip

This dish is perfect for a party. Keep this on low heat, and the last bite will be as good as the first. The use of crabmeat brings a gourmet flair. To me, it just shows a person who has good taste.

16 ounces cream cheese
8 ounces shredded pepper jack cheese
2 teaspoons Worcestershire sauce
1 1/2 cups green onion, chopped
1/4 cup fresh parsley, chopped
1/2 cup half & half
1 pound crabmeat, picked thru for shells
Creole Seasoning Blend to taste (page 146)

Combine cheeses, Worcestershire sauce, green onion, parsley, and half & half in a medium saucepan. Cook over low heat until the dip reaches desired consistency. Add crabmeat and Creole seasoning. Cook for 3 minutes. Serve with crackers.

Hot Crawfish Dip

Most of the time, I prefer eating crawfish instead of lobster (not that I would *ever* turn down a lobster dinner). I like crawfish because they are made to be eaten spicy. I have always wanted to boil a lobster, crawfish style, but I think the lobster would lose its sweetness. This is a dish you could substitute lobster for crawfish.

1 onion, diced
1 green bell pepper, diced
3 stalks, celery, diced
1 garlic clove, minced
1 pound crawfish tails, chopped
1/2 cup butter
8 ounces cream cheese
1/4 cup mayonnaise
1 teaspoon dry mustard
Salt, black pepper to taste
Creole Seasoning Blend to taste (page 146)
1 tablespoon fresh parsley chopped

Sauté bell pepper, onions, celery, garlic and crawfish in butter. Add cream cheese, lower temperature and cover to let cream cheese melt. Add mayonnaise, salt, pepper, Creole seasoning to taste. Simmer approximately 15-20 minutes. Add parsley. Serve warm.

Marinated Crab Claws

This is one of my favorite cold dishes. It seems that the longer you allow the crab claws to marinate, the better they taste. This is a dish that you want some bread to dip into the sauce. I wish it were crab season year-round.

1/2 cup extra-virgin olive oil
1/3 cup water
1/4 cup red wine vinegar
1 tablespoon lemon juice
1/4 cup garlic, chopped
1/4 cup green onion, chopped

1/4 cup fresh parsley, chopped
3 tablespoons Worcestershire sauce
1 tablespoon fresh thyme, chopped
1 tablespoon fresh basil, chopped
1/4 teaspoon salt
1/4 teaspoon black pepper
1 1/2 teaspoon hot sauce
1 pound crab claws peeled

In a large mixing bowl, add olive oil, water, vinegar, lemon juice, garlic, green onion, parsley, and Worcestershire sauce. With a wire whisk, mix all ingredients until they are well blended. Add herbs and remaining seasonings. Add crab claws and coat well with seasoning mixture. Cover and refrigerate overnight.

Natchitoches Meat Pies

A Natchitoches meat pie is Louisiana's answer to the Central American empanada. Natchitoches is located in the North Central part of Louisiana. It was made famous in the movie Steel Magnolias, but I think that the meat pie is their real claim to fame. A soft flaky dough filled with seasoned meat, deep fried to perfection. I can taste one right now.

1 tablespoon vegetable oil
1 tablespoon flour
1/2 cup onion, minced
1/4 cup celery, minced
1/4 cup green bell pepper, minced
1 clove garlic, minced
1 pound ground beef
1/2 pound ground pork
1 teaspoon *Creole Seasoning Blend* (page 146)
1 (15oz) package refrigerated pie dough at room temperature

Preheat deep fryer to 375°F.

Heat oil in a large skillet over medium low heat. Whisk in flour and cook until it is a nutty brown color, 2-3 minutes. Stir in vegetables and cook until soft and onions are transparent, about 5 minutes. Add meats and brown until no longer pink, about 10 minutes. Stir in Creole seasoning and drain the fat. Cool to room temperature. On a lightly floured surface, roll out the dough to a thickness of 1/4 inch. Use a 5-inch cookie cutter to cut circles in the dough. Place a heaping tablespoon of the meat mixture and put it in the center of the dough round. Fold the dough over and seal the edges using a fork. You may need to reroll the dough scraps to make 15 meat pies. Deep fry pies in small batches until golden brown, about 3-4 minutes. Drain on paper towels and serve while hot.

Oysters Bienville

Oysters Bienville is often served as part of Oysters 2-2-2, which is 2 Oysters Rockefeller, 2 Oysters Bienville and 2 of the restaurant's own oyster creation. But Oysters Bienville is a dish that can stand on its own. It is as rich as Oysters Rockefeller but not as popular. Combining oysters with shrimp on a half shell makes a mini seafood combo platter. In my opinion, they are better than Oysters Rockefeller.

Rock salt
2 strips of bacon, finely chopped
1/2 cup onion, chopped
1/4 teaspoon *Seafood Seasoning Blend* (page 148)
1/2 teaspoon garlic, chopped
1 tablespoon butter
1 1/2 tablespoons flour
1/2 cup half and half
1/4 cup Chablis wine
1/4 cup mushrooms, finely chopped
1/4 pound medium shrimp, peeled, deveined and coarsely chopped
1 tablespoon Parmesan cheese, grated
1 tablespoon Romano cheese, grated
2 teaspoons lemon juice
2 tablespoons green onion, chopped, tops only
2 teaspoons fresh parsley leaves, chopped
1 egg yolk, slightly beaten
1 dozen oysters in their half shell
Preheat oven to 400°F.

Spread rock salt on a large baking pan. Fry bacon until crisp in a medium skillet over medium-high heat. Add onions and seafood seasoning; cook, stirring for 2 minutes. Add garlic and butter, and cook while stirring, until the butter melts. Add flour and cook for 2 minutes stirring constantly. Add half and half and wine; stir to blend. Reduce the heat to medium, add mushrooms and shrimp. Stir and fold to mix and cook until the mixture is thick, about 3-4 minutes. Add cheeses, lemon juice, green onions, and parsley. Stir to blend. Remove from heat. Add egg yolk and blend well. Let cool to room temperature. Arrange the shells on the rock salt. Make sure they do not move. Put one oyster in each shell and top with 1 1/2 tablespoons of the sauce. Make sure the sauce is spread out to the edges of the shell and covers the oyster completely. Bake until sauce is golden brown and oysters begin to curl around the edges, about 20 minutes.

Carefully transfer to plates with rock salt to keep the oysters from moving. Serve immediately.

Oysters Centola

Oysters Mosca is a wonderful Creole Italian creation. For over 60 years, Mosca's restaurant has existed twenty minutes from downtown New Orleans in the town of Waggaman on the west bank of the river. Most people in New Orleans have their own version of this dish. So, here is mine. I add a couple of ingredients that make this dish unique. The first is tasso, a seasoned piece of pork shoulder. The second is sriracha, a hot chili sauce found in the Asian section in the grocery store.

4 tablespoons butter, melted
1/2 cup olive oil
1 tablespoon fresh garlic, chopped
1½ teaspoons sriracha
1/3 cup tasso, diced
1 pint oysters
1 tablespoon fresh parsley, chopped
1 tablespoon fresh basil, chopped
3/4 cup Italian bread crumbs
3/4 cup Parmesan cheese, freshly grated

Preheat oven to 400°F. Combine butter and olive oil in a 9x9-inch baking pan. Stir in garlic, sriracha and tasso. Layer oysters in the pan. In a separate bowl, combine parsley, basil, breadcrumbs, and Parmesan cheese. Sprinkle the breadcrumb mixture over the oysters making sure they are totally covered. Bake for 20 minutes. Serve immediately. You can also put these into individual dishes for ease of serving.

Oysters en Brochette

In my opinion, Galatoire's Restaurant, on Bourbon Street in the French Quarter, prepares this dish better than any other restaurant. The pairing of oysters with bacon is a match made in heaven. Topped with a meunière sauce, this is a great way to start any meal.

1 pound bacon, cut into 3-inch strips
4 wooden skewers (6 inch) soaked in water
24 oysters
2 cups *Seafood Breading* (page 148)
Egg Wash (page 147)
Meunière Sauce (page 109)

Preheat deep fryer to 375°F. Place one piece of bacon on the skewer and follow it with an oyster. Continue this process until there are 6 oysters on the skewer and there are bacon strips on both ends. Dip the skewer in the egg wash. Drain, and then dredge them in the breading, shaking off the excess. Fry for 2-3 minutes or until golden brown. Drain on a paper towel. Top with meunière sauce and serve.

Pomme Soufflé

This is the ultimate french fry. There are a few stories as to how they were invented. One involves a king who loved french fries and had asked for his dinner to be delayed 30 minutes. The chef had already started cooking the potatoes, so he pulled them out of the oil and let them drain. When the king was ready to eat, the chef put them back into the oil and they puffed up. Pomme soufflé became the king's favorite dish.

You need to cook the potatoes twice, once at 325°F and once in 375°F. You need to cut the potatoes in slices 1/4 to 3/4 inch thick. Soak the sliced potatoes in ice water for at least 25 minutes. Drain and dry them thoroughly. You want to cook the potatoes the first time, 325°F, for 6-7 minutes occasionally moving the potatoes around. Drain them on paper towels until they begin to soften. At this point, you can cook them the second time, 375°F, or hold them at room temperature for several hours until service. Serve these with béarnaise sauce for dipping (See Lagniappe section for recipe).

Seafood Crêpes

New Orleans is blessed being surrounded by water filled with wonderful seafood. This dish celebrates the French. The French will stuff a crêpe with almost anything. Of course, in New Orleans, seafood is the filling of choice. You can use any fresh seafood in the dish. If you are afraid of making crêpes, most grocery stores sell them already made.

Crêpe Batter (page 146)
4 tablespoons butter
1/3 cup onion, finely chopped
2 tablespoons dry vermouth
3 tablespoons flour
1 1/2 cups plus 2 tablespoons milk, divided
1 cup cooked shrimp, peeled, deveined and coarsely chopped
1 cup lump crabmeat, picked over for shells
1 cup crawfish tails, coarsely chopped
2 tablespoons fresh parsley, chopped
3 tablespoons fresh Parmesan cheese, grated

Preheat oven to 350°F.

Grease a 13x9-inch baking pan. In a medium saucepan, melt butter over medium heat. Add onion and cook until tender and translucent, about 5 minutes. Add vermouth and cook another minute. Stir in flour and cook for 1 minute, constantly stirring. Gradually stir in 1 1/2 of milk. Bring to a boil, stirring frequently. Reduce heat to low and simmer until the sauce thickens. Remove from heat and stir in the seafood. Reserve 1/2 cup of the seafood mixture. To assemble the crêpes, spoon about 1/4 cup of the seafood mixture down the center of the crêpe. Roll up the crêpes and place them seam side down in the pan. Stir parsley and remaining 2 tablespoons of milk into the reserved seafood mixture. Spoon the mixture down the center of the crêpe and sprinkle with the Parmesan cheese. Bake uncovered 15 to 20 minutes or until heated through. Serve immediately.

Shrimp Rehoboth

This is a dish that I have played around with for about 15 years. I found that the ingredient I was looking for is sriracha. Just two drops of the hot chili sauce make the dish. As far as the name of the dish, Rehoboth is the street on which I live.

Sweet Red Dressing
1/2 cup sugar
1/4 teaspoon onion salt
1/2 cup ketchup
1/2 cup cider vinegar
1/2 cup vegetable oil
2 drops of sriracha sauce

Combine all ingredients.
8 julienne strips green bell pepper
8 julienne strips red bell pepper
8 julienne strips red onion

Sweet Red Dressing
1 tablespoon butter
24 raw medium shrimp, peeled
2 teaspoons *Creole Seasoning Blend* (page 146)

Marinate vegetables in ½ cup of the sweet red dressing. Over medium heat, melt butter in a large sauté pan. Sprinkle Creole seasoning over the shrimp and toss to coat. Add shrimp and vegetables to the pan and sauté until the shrimp are almost done, about 4 minutes. Add the rest of the red dressing and cook until the sauce is warm, coating the shrimp and vegetables.

Spinach Dip

This is the recipe most people request for me to make when we have get-togethers. This is my take on Cannon's restaurant most popular appetizer. Many times, people have told me that they do not like spinach but love the spinach dip. These are best served with plain tortilla chips. This is a great way to say, "Hey, Mom! I am eating my spinach."

3 ounces butter
1/3 cup olive oil
1 cup onion, chopped
1 3/4 tablespoon garlic, minced
1/2 cup plus 2 tablespoons flour
1 pint heavy cream
1 pint *Chicken Stock* (page 146)
1 teaspoon salt
1 1/2 teaspoons sugar
2 tablespoons lemon juice
1/4 teaspoon cayenne pepper
1 1/4 cup Parmesan cheese, grated
1 cup sour cream
1 teaspoon Tabasco sauce
3 pounds spinach, chopped
1 cup artichoke hearts, chopped

Add butter and olive oil to a 5-quart pan and heat over medium heat. Do not burn butter. Add the onions and garlic. Sauté until onions are soft. Turn down heat and add flour to make a roux. Cook slowly for 5 minutes. Do not allow roux to brown. Slowly add cream and chicken stock to roux. Bring to a simmer and cook for 5 minutes. Add salt, sugar, lemon juice, cayenne pepper and cheese to mixture and remove from heat. When the sauce has slightly cooled, add sour cream and tabasco. Add spinach and artichoke hearts to sauce and reheat before serving.

Stuffed Artichokes

This is one of my mother's most asked-for recipe. It is a very easy recipe to make. The key is finding large enough artichokes to use all of the stuffing. It is Creole Italian cooking at its finest.

2 artichokes
1 cup Italian bread crumbs
1 cup Parmesan cheese, grated
1 teaspoon dried parsley
1 teaspoon Italian seasoning
4 cloves garlic chopped
1/3 cup olive oil

Boil artichokes for 45 minutes. Preheat oven to 350°F. Mix the dry ingredients. Saturate the dry mixture with the olive oil. Stuff the leaves of the artichoke. Bake, covered with foil for 1 1/2 hours in a large dish with 1 inch of water in it, to keep the stuffing from drying out.

Stuffed Mushrooms

This is one of my wife's favorite appetizers. She orders it every time we go to Copeland's restaurant. Most people like to use lump crabmeat in every dish. While this adds to the eye appeal of a dish, you do not get as much crab flavor than when you use claw meat. Claw meat is dark and stringy; however, it has the most flavor. It is the perfect crabmeat for stuffed mushrooms.

1 pound button mushrooms, large
Non-stick butter spray
6 tablespoons butter, divided
1/4 cup green onion, minced
1/4 cup red bell peppers, minced
8 ounces claw crabmeat
1 cup Italian bread crumbs
2 cloves garlic, minced
1/2 teaspoon *Creole Seasoning Blend* (page 146)
2 tablespoons Parmesan cheese, grated

Heat oven to 350°F.

Wash and trim the end of the stem of the mushrooms. Pop the remaining stem out. Chop the stems and set aside. Spray an 8x8-inch baking pan with butter spray. Layer mushrooms in the pan. Melt 2 tablespoons of the butter and brush over the mushrooms. Melt the remaining butter in a medium skillet.

Add the reserved mushroom stems, green onions and red bell pepper, cooking them until they are tender. Combine the cooked ingredients with crabmeat, breadcrumbs, garlic, and Creole seasoning. Fill each mushroom and sprinkle with Parmesan cheese. Bake for 15 to 20 minutes, until hot and mushroom caps are tender.

VooDoo Rolls

One day, I was wondering what to do with leftover crawfish tails. I wanted to try something different but did not know what. I was in the produce section of the grocery when I saw egg roll wrappers. With a big grin, I took some home to work with, and soon, I had the following recipe.

2 teaspoons *Creole Seasoning Blend* (page 146)
10 ounces crawfish tails
1/4 cup onion, minced
3 cloves garlic, minced
6 ounces andouille sausage cut in a small dice
5 tablespoons Worcestershire sauce

8 ounces mozzarella cheese, shredded
20 Egg Roll Wrappers

Put Creole seasoning on crawfish and toss to cover. Sauté onion and garlic in Worcestershire sauce for 2 minutes. Add crawfish and andouille. Sauté for 3 minutes. Drain and allow to cool. Mix cheese with the cool meat mixture. Place egg roll wrapper on a dry surface. Place 2 tablespoons of the meat and cheese mixture in a roll in the middle of the wrapper. Fold the sides of the wrapper 1/2 inch over the mixture. Wet one end and roll it toward that end. Press to seal. Fry rolls at 375°F until golden, about 2 minutes. Make sure to turn the rolls so that both sides cook evenly.

Soups

Everyone knows that New Orleans is famous for gumbo. Often, people have a bowl of seafood gumbo and some French bread as their meal. Now, you would think that with the heat and humidity in the city, soups would not be a popular seller. With all the flavor found in New Orleans' soups, one does not want to miss all of its deliciousness. Oyster and artichoke soup is a very rich soup, but no one pushes the dish away until every drop is gone. There are some soups--oyster soup, Creole French onion soup, and turtle soup--which do not contain milk or cream. These are for those days when you want something hot but not too heavy. But in New Orleans, there is no such thing as a dish that is too rich.

Asparagus
Broccoli and Cheese
Chicken and Mushroom
Chicken and Sausage Gumbo
Crab Bisque
Crawfish Bisque
Creole Onion Soup
Gumbo Z'Herbs
Oyster and Artichoke
Oyster Rockefeller Soup
Oyster Soup
Potato Soup
Red Bean Soup
Shrimp and Corn Chowder

Asparagus Soup

Asparagus is a spring vegetable. At Cannon's restaurant, we would serve this soup for three or four months of the year. If not for the price and quality of asparagus out of season, this soup would have people waiting in line throughout the year. Come spring, we would start getting requests for this crowd pleaser.

1 stick butter
1 pound onions, chopped
2/3 cup flour
1 teaspoon salt
1/2 teaspoon white pepper
1 bay leaf
1 1/2 quarts + 2/3 cup *Chicken Stock* (page 146)
1 teaspoon *Creole Seasoning Blend* (page 146)
1 pound fresh steamed asparagus
1 pint + 1 cup heavy cream

Melt butter. Sauté onions until transparent. Add flour, salt, pepper, bay leaf, chicken stock, and Creole seasoning to pan. Reduce by half and thicken to desired consistency.

Take 1 pint of stock out of the pot. Put portions of steamed asparagus in blender with enough stock to allow the blender to spin freely. Pour blended asparagus in a separate container until all asparagus is blended. Add blended asparagus and remaining stock to pot. Blend well. Add heavy cream and allow to thicken.

Broccoli & Cheese Soup

Mothers would do anything to get children to eat their broccoli. Someone melted some cheese on top of fresh steamed broccoli. Someone took it a step further, and the result is below. While broccoli is good for you, do not kid yourself into thinking this soup is healthy. But that is what makes it so good.

1/4 pound margarine (1 stick)
2 cups broccoli minced (buds and stems)
1 cup onion, chopped
1/2 cup flour
3/4 quart *Chicken Stock* (page 146)
3/4 quart half and half
1 tablespoon parsley flakes
1 1/2 pounds Velveeta cheese

Melt margarine. Sauté broccoli and onion until soft. Add flour and mix well. Slowly add chicken stock stirring with a wire whisk. On a low fire, cook out the flour taste for approximately 5 minutes. Pour in half and half with a steady flow, stirring continuously. Cook 5 more minutes. Add Velveeta slowly. Cook approximately 10 minutes.

Chicken & Mushroom Soup

This is another favorite from Cannon's restaurant. We had customers who would only eat there on the day this soup was served. There was even a customer who asked to have the mushrooms taken out before it was brought to the table. He did not like mushrooms but loved the soup too much to do without.

4 tablespoons margarine
1 quart fresh mushrooms, cut stems & buttons
1/2 pound butter (2 sticks)
1 cup onion, chopped
3/4 cup flour
1 3/4 cups *Chicken Stock* (page 146)
1 quart cooked chicken breast, diced small
1 tablespoon lemon juice
1 1/2 cups heavy cream
1/4 teaspoon ground white pepper
1/2 teaspoon thyme
1 teaspoon tarragon leaves
Pinch nutmeg

Sauté mushrooms in margarine. Remove from heat and save mushrooms, discard margarine. Melt butter and sauté onion over medium heat. Do not brown onions. Add flour and cook for 2-3 minutes. Add chicken stock slowly, mixing with a wire whisk to keep flour from lumping. Cook flour taste out and let thicken until it resembles creamy mashed potatoes in consistency. Add chicken and mushrooms. Cook for 10 minutes. Add lemon juice. Stir in heavy cream and cook for 10 minutes. Add white pepper, thyme, tarragon, and nutmeg. Pull off heat and serve.

Chicken and Sausage Gumbo

Chicken and sausage gumbo has been around for a long time. When Mr. B's restaurant, located in the French Quarter opened, they called their gumbo Gumbo Ya Ya. This gumbo tends to be thinner than a seafood gumbo. But the taste is just as good. This gumbo is great when fresh seafood is not available.

5 pounds chicken meat, medium dice
2 tablespoons *Creole Seasoning Blend* (page 146)
2 1/2 cups flour
1 cup vegetable oil

2 cups onion, chopped
1 1/2 cups celery, chopped
2 cups green bell pepper, chopped
6 cups *Chicken Stock* (page 146)
1 1/2 tablespoons garlic, minced
1 1/2 pounds andouille sausage, cut into small discs
4 cups rice, cooked and hot

Season chicken with Creole seasoning blend and let stand at room temperature for 20 minutes. Measure flour into a large paper bag. Add chicken and shake until well coated. Remove chicken and set remaining flour aside. In a large skillet, brown chicken in very hot oil. When browned, remove chicken and set aside. Stir oil remaining in the skillet with a wire whisk to loosen any brown bits remaining on the bottom of the pan. Whisk in 1 cup of the remaining flour and whisk constantly over medium heat until the roux becomes dark brown. Be sure to stir constantly and do not let this mixture burn. If it burns, you must start the roux over. It will probably take 15-25 minutes. Add onion, celery and bell pepper, cooking until the vegetables are tender. Transfer roux and vegetables to a large heavy saucepan. Add stock to the roux and bring to a boil, stirring occasionally. Lower heat to a quick simmer and add the garlic, sausage and chicken. Continue cooking, covered, until the chicken is tender, 1 3/4-2 hours. Adjust seasonings and serve in bowls over rice.

Crab Bisque

This is not the traditional crab bisque you would find in New Orleans. It is made along the lines of lobster bisque. This is a creamy bisque, not a tomato-based bisque. I love lobster bisque and thought the change to crab meat would make a good copy. To my surprise, I liked it better than the lobster bisque. You decide.

2 tablespoons butter
1 teaspoon onion, minced
1 1/2 cups crabmeat, cleaned
1 tablespoon fresh parsley, chopped
2 teaspoons flour
2 cups crab stock or *Seafood Stock* (page 149)
2 cups heavy cream
Pinch ground white pepper
Salt

In a saucepan, melt butter. Add the onion and cook until golden. Add crabmeat and parsley: cook over low heat stirring consistently (about 4 minutes). Add flour, stir to blend and cook for three minutes. Stir in crab stock and simmer gently for 20 minutes. Keep pan partially covered. Add the cream and white pepper. Heat and add salt to taste.

Crawfish Bisque

This is a traditional interpretation of crawfish bisque. Made with a roux and tomato sauce, this dish is very different than lobster bisque. Sometimes, you will find stuffed crawfish heads served with this dish. The crawfish heads are cleaned out and stuffed with a breadcrumb Parmesan cheese mixture. You get one teaspoon of stuffing per head. To me, eating a stuffed crawfish head is more work than necessary. If you want to eat something out of a crawfish shell, just boil crawfish.

1 cup canola oil
1 cup flour
1 cup onion, diced
1/2 cup bell pepper, diced
1/2 cup celery, diced
2 1/2 tablespoons garlic, minced
1/4 cup tomato sauce
3 quarts *Seafood Stock,* room temperature (page 149)
1 tablespoon *Creole Seasoning Blend* (page 146)
1 pound crawfish tails
1 cup green onion, diced
1/2 cup fresh parsley, chopped
Cooked rice

In a heavy 6-quart pot, heat oil over medium heat. Stir in flour, stirring constantly, until you get a dark roux. Add onion, bell pepper, celery, and garlic. Sauté until vegetables are soft and translucent. Add tomato sauce and stir. Add stock slowly, stirring well to incorporate with the roux. Add Creole seasoning and stir. Cover and reduce heat, simmering for 30 minutes. Stir in crawfish tails, green onion and parsley; cover, and simmer for 5 more minutes. Serve in a bowl over rice.

Creole Onion Soup

My favorite version of this soup is from the now-closed LeRuth's restaurant. It was not unusual to have a cup or two while working. The visual of that first spoonful is burnt into my memory: a combination of soup and bread with melted cheese stretching until it broke. One taste was sure to make you want more.

1 loaf French bread
1/2 stick butter
1 yellow onion, sliced thinly
1 red onion, sliced thinly
1/4 cup flour
1/4 teaspoon black pepper
1/4 teaspoon garlic powder

1/2 teaspoon *Creole Seasoning Blend* (page 146)
1/4 cup tomato sauce
2 tablespoons soy sauce
21 ounces beef stock
1 cup shredded Swiss cheese

Heat oven to 325°F.

Slice bread one-inch thick and place on rack in the oven; remove bread when golden brown. In a saucepan over medium heat, melt butter. Cook onions in butter, stirring, until golden, about 15 minutes. Sprinkle in flour, pepper, garlic powder, and Creole seasoning over onions and continue to cook until flour is golden brown, as well. Stir in tomato sauce and soy sauce. Cook one minute more. Stir in the beef broth and simmer 10 minutes, or until onions reach the desired consistency. Pour soup into ovenproof bowls. Place a piece of French bread in each bowl and top with Swiss cheese. When cheese has melted, serve at once.

Gumbo Z'Herbs

Gumbo Z'herbs, or Green Gumbo, is a dish that is traditionally served during Lent. Each Holy Thursday, Leah Chase, owner of Dooky Chase's restaurant, served what is considered the best version of this dish. This dish was prepared by the Creoles on Holy Thursday as the last big "meat" meal before Easter Sunday. It is said that if you eat this dish on Holy Thursday, you will have as many new friends as there are greens used in the Gumbo. The number of greens used must be uneven. This one contains nine.

1 bunch mustard greens
1 bunch collard greens
1 bunch turnips
1 bunch watercress
1 bunch beet tops
1 bunch carrot tops
1/2 head lettuce
1/2 head cabbage
1 bunch spinach
3 cups onion, diced
3/4 cups garlic
1 1/2 gallons water
5 tablespoons flour
1 pound smoked sausage, diced
1 pound smoked ham, diced
1 pound hot sausage, diced
1 pound brisket, cubed
1 pound stew meat

1 1/2 teaspoon thyme
Salt and cayenne pepper to taste
1 tablespoon filé powder
Hot cooked rice

Clean all greens under cold water, making sure to pick out bad leaves. Rinse away any soil or dirt. The greens should be washed 3 times. Chop greens coarsely and place in a 12-quart pot along with the onion, garlic and water. Bring mixture to a rolling boil. Reduce the heat to simmer. Cover and cook for 30 minutes. Strain greens and reserve the liquid. Place greens in the bowl of a food processor and puree. Pour greens into a mixing bowl, sprinkle in the flour. Blend and set aside. Place meats into the 12-quart pot. Return the reserve liquid to the pot and bring to a low boil. Cover and cook for 30 minutes. Add pureed greens, thyme and season with salt and cayenne. Cover and continue to simmer, stirring occasionally until the meat is tender, approximately one hour. Add water if necessary to retain volume. Add the filé powder and stir well. Serve over hot cooked rice.

Oyster and Artichoke Soup

It is said that Chef Warren Leruth of LeRuth's restaurant created oyster and artichoke soup. This soup was the house special. Many restaurants have tried to copy this soup. Chef Leruth once said that there is no cream in his soup. It is magic what this man was able to do. I guess that is why I gravitated to the restaurant business, hoping to create some magic of my own.

3 sticks butter
1 cup onion diced
1 cup green onion, chopped
3/4 cup flour
1/2 gallon *Chicken Stock* (page 146)
6 cups quartered artichoke hearts (reserve liquid)
3 tablespoons lemon juice
3/4 cup grated Parmesan cheese
1/2 tablespoon Worcestershire sauce
1/2 teaspoon hot sauce
1/2 tablespoon oregano
1/2 teaspoon thyme
1/2 teaspoon salt
1/2 tablespoon white pepper
1 tablespoon granulated garlic
2 tablespoons light brown sugar
1 quart oysters, chopped

Melt butter and sauté onion until transparent. Add green onion and sauté for 2 minutes. Mix chicken stock and artichoke juice. Add flour to onions and stir with a wire whisk. Cook for 2 minutes. Add stock mixture and stir. Add artichokes, lemon juice and Parmesan cheese; stir. Add Worcestershire sauce, hot sauce, oregano, thyme, salt, white pepper, granulated garlic, and brown sugar, sprinkling all of the ingredients over the entire area of soup to avoid clumping. Cook for 10 minutes on low temperature. Add oysters and cook for 5 minutes.

Oysters Rockefeller Soup

This is a great way to make Oysters Rockefeller for a large group. Also, if you are unable to get your oysters in their shell, you can serve them in a soup. I find that this soup makes Oysters Rockefeller richer than the original dish. Either way, you will feel like a million bucks eating Oysters Rockefeller.

1 pint shucked oysters
2 quarts cold water
1 1/2 sticks butter
3/4 cup celery, chopped
1/2 cup flour
8 ounces fresh spinach leaves, washed, stemmed and coarsely chopped
1/2 cup fresh parsley, finely chopped
2 teaspoons fresh thyme, finely chopped
1/2 teaspoon *Creole Seasoning Blend* (page 146)
2 cups heavy cream

Place oysters in a large saucepan and cover with 2 quarts cold water. Cook over medium heat just until the oysters begin to curl, about 5 minutes. Strain the oysters, reserving the stock. Set the oysters aside. Melt butter in a large pot and sauté the celery until tender. Stir in the flour, and then add the oysters and oyster stock. Reduce the heat and simmer for 10 minutes, or until thickened. Add spinach, parsley, thyme and Creole seasoning. Pour in the cream and simmer several minutes until the soup is hot.

Oyster Soup

With oyster season traditionally being in the months with Rs in them, this soup is great for taking off the chill. Most oyster soups contain milk or cream. This one contains neither, so you can get more of the oyster flavor. You could always add some milk or cream when adding the last ingredients.

1/2 pound butter
2 cups celery, finely chopped
1 cup green onion, finely chopped
1 1/4 cup flour

2 tablespoons garlic, minced
4 bay leaves
1 teaspoon white pepper
4 dozen large oysters, freshly shucked*
12 cups oyster water (oyster liquid and enough water to make 12 cups)
2 teaspoon salt

Melt butter over medium heat in a 6-quart heavy saucepan. Sauté celery and green onion until tender but not browned, stirring frequently. Gradually stir in the flour and cook 5 minutes longer, stirring constantly over low heat. Add the remaining ingredients and simmer for 20 minutes. Remove the pan from heat and discard the bay leaves. Serve immediately.

* If you get oysters that are already shucked, use the liquid in which they were packed.

Potato Soup

This is one of the most popular soups seen on restaurant menus today. This is a good soup but unless I make it, I feel something is missing. The trick: boil the potatoes like they were prepared in a seafood boil. My key ingredient is liquid crab boil. Adding this to the boiling water gives the soup a little extra pop.

Potatoes (6-8 depending on the size)
2 ounces liquid crab boil
1/2 pound butter
1/2 cup onion, diced
3/4 cup flour
7 cups *Chicken Stock* (page 146)
2 cups water
1/4 teaspoon salt
1/4 teaspoon pepper
1/8 teaspoon dry basil
1/8 teaspoon sugar
1 1/2 heavy cream

Put the potatoes in a large pot and cover with enough water to reach 3 inches above the potatoes. Add crab boil. Boil the potatoes, peel and set aside. In a large soup pot, melt butter over a medium low heat. Add onion and cook until softened. Add the flour and cook for 3 minutes, stirring constantly. Slowly add chicken stock, water, salt, pepper, basil, and sugar. Bring to a boil, stirring often with a wire whisk. Gradually add the heavy cream until you have reached the desired consistency. Chop potatoes into bite-sized cubes and add to the soup. Simmer for approximately 5 minutes to bring the potatoes to temperature. If you wish, you can garnish the soup with chopped bacon, chopped chives and shredded cheese.

CHEF TOMMY CENTOLA

Red Bean Soup

This is another soup that is a version of a traditional New Orleans dish. Red beans are a staple on Mondays. Most places offer this on other days of the week. That way, people do not have to wait for Monday to have red beans.

1 tablespoon olive oil
8 ounces bacon, cooked and chopped
1 1/2 cups onion, chopped
1/4 cup green bell pepper, chopped
1 tablespoon garlic, minced
3 bay leaves
8 ounces andouille sausage, sliced into bite sized disc
2 cups dry kidney beans, soaked overnight
1 teaspoon *Creole Seasoning Blend* (page 146)
1 teaspoon Worcestershire sauce
8 cups *Chicken Stock* (page 146)
1 teaspoon salt
Cooked rice

In a large pot over high heat, heat the oil. Add bacon and sauté for 2 minutes. Add onion, bell pepper, garlic, bay leaves, and andouille and sauté 2 more minutes. Add beans and sauté for 2 minutes more. Stir in Creole seasoning, Worcestershire sauce and stock. Bring to a boil. Reduce heat to low and simmer for 1 hour, stirring occasionally. Add salt, cover the pot, and simmer for an additional 15 minutes. Turn off the heat and allow the pot to sit, covered, for about 20 minutes. Serve with 1/4 cup of cooked rice.

Shrimp and Corn Chowder

This hearty soup is great on those cold winter days. The shrimp and corn complement each other's sweetness. This soup is also quick to prepare. You can have it ready in 45 minutes. If you want to add a special touch to a winter's night meal, this is the perfect addition to your menu. You can also substitute crawfish for the shrimp.

4 slice bacon, diced into 1-inch pieces
1/3 cup onion, diced
3 tablespoons flour, divided
8 ounces *Seafood Stock* or clam juice (page 149)
1 cup plus 2 tablespoons water, divided
2 medium red potatoes, peeled and diced
2 celery stalks, diced
1 bay leaf

2 teaspoons salt
2 teaspoons *Creole Seasoning Blend* (page 146)
2 cups whole milk
1 pound medium shrimp, peeled and deveined
1 cup frozen corn

In a large Dutch oven, cook bacon until browned. Reserve 1 1/2 tablespoon of the bacon drippings. Set bacon aside. Add onion to the Dutch oven with the reserved bacon drippings. Cook until soft, about 5 minutes. Sprinkle with 2 tablespoons of flour. Cook for 2 minutes. Pour stock and water into Dutch oven. Add potatoes, celery, bay leaf, salt, and Creole seasoning. Bring to a boil. Reduce heat and cook until the potatoes are tender. Stir in 3 tablespoons of hot broth into the milk to temper it. Pour tempered milk into the soup. Make a slurry with the remaining 1-tablespoon of flour and 2 tablespoons of water. Stir slurry into soup and let simmer for 30 more minutes. After the soup has simmered, add the shrimp and corn. Cook 5 minutes more or until the shrimp are pink and cooked through. Remove bay leaf. Stir in the reserve bacon. Serve immediately.

Salads And Dressings

You would think that salads would be popular in New Orleans. The heat in the summertime makes most people eat lighter dishes; however, most New Orleanians satisfy their salad course with shrimp remoulade. With the introduction of newer greens, salads have started to make an impression on New Orleans diners; and nothing tops salads better than homemade dressing. I have included several dressing recipes that are delicious on almost any salad. Salad recipes are family sized.

Caesar Salad
Cajun Popcorn Salad
Fried Oyster Caesar
Godchaux Salad
Muffuletta Salad
Oriental Chicken Salad
Perry St. Pasta Salad
Uptown Salad
Warm Spinach Salad
1000 Island Dressing
Bleu Cheese Dressing
Caesar Dressing
Honey Mustard Dressing
Hot Bacon Dressing
Thai Peanut Vinaigrette
Vinaigrette

Caesar Salad

This salad was created in Mexico on the Fourth of July 1924. Caesar Cardini, an Italian-born Mexican, invented the dish. When a rush in the restaurant caused a depletion of supplies, Caesar got creative with the items he had on hand. He also prepared the salad table side to the delight of his guest.

2 heads romaine lettuce, cleaned and chopped into bite sized pieces
6 ounces *Caesar Dressing* (page 64)
2 cups croutons
4 ounces shredded Parmesan cheese

Put romaine in a large mixing bowl. Add dressing and toss until lettuce is well coated. Put into serving bowls and top with croutons and Parmesan cheese. Serves four dinner salads or eight side salads.

Cajun Popcorn Salad

Cannon's Restaurant created the Cajun popcorn salad. This dish was so popular, it accounted for a significant percentage of the entrees that were sold. The crunchiness of the fried shrimp combined with lettuce and honey mustard dressing was unbeatable. It was served with a piece of French bread topped with melted cheese.

32 ounces small raw shrimp, peeled and deveined
Cajun Popcorn Batter (page 144)
2 heads iceberg lettuce, cleaned and cut into bite sized pieces
1 head romaine lettuce, cleaned and cut into bite sized pieces
1/4 cup carrot, shredded
1/4 cup red cabbage, shredded
12 ounces *Honey Mustard Dressing* (page 65)

Preheat deep fryer to 360°F. Mix together lettuce, carrot and cabbage. Put the lettuce mixture into four chilled bowls. Top each salad with 3 ounces of honey mustard dressing. Dip shrimp into popcorn batter and shake off the excess. Drop into fryer, spreading them out to avoid clumping. Fry for 2-3 minutes, then drain on paper towels. Top each salad with equal amounts of the popcorn shrimp. Feeds four.

Fried Oyster Caesar Salad

This is a great light salad for lunch. You can be happy that you are eating a healthy salad, while eating delicious fried oysters. The oysters replace the croutons on a traditional Caesar Salad.

32 raw oysters

Seafood Breading (page 148)
Egg Wash (page 147)
2 heads romaine lettuce, cleaned and chopped into bite sized pieces
6 ounces *Caesar Dressing* (page 64)
4 ounces shredded Parmesan cheese

Heat deep fryer to 360°F. Dip oysters into the egg wash, then dredge in seafood batter. Shake off excess batter and fry for 2-3 minutes. Put romaine in a large mixing bowl. Add dressing and toss until lettuce is well coated. Put into four serving bowls and top with fried oysters and Parmesan cheese. Feeds four.

Godchaux Salad

Godchaux's was a New Orleans Department store on Canal Street. In the 1920s, Leon Godchaux would walk to Galatoire's restaurant in the French Quarter of New Orleans for lunch. During the warm months, Mr. Godchaux would ask for a salad made with all of his favorite things. Over the years, this dish became a popular addition to Galatoire's menu.

1 head iceberg lettuce, cleaned and cut into large ribbons
2 large tomatoes, cored and cleaned
1 pound lump crabmeat, picked through for shells
36 large shrimp, boiled and peeled
2/3 cup salad oil
1/3 cup red wine vinegar
1/2 cup Creole mustard
3 eggs, hard boiled and chopped
12 anchovy filets

In a large salad bowl, combine lettuce, tomatoes, crabmeat, and shrimp. In a small bowl, combine oil, vinegar and Creole mustard: whisk together to create the dressing. Pour dressing over the salad and toss. Divide salad into six chilled plates or bowls. Garnish each salad with chopped eggs and 2 anchovy filets. Feeds six.

Muffuletta Salad

This is a lighter way to enjoy a muffuletta. By taking the insides of a muffuletta and putting them on a bed of lettuce, you have made the ultimate Creole Italian Salad. With the olive oil mixture from the olive salad, there is no need for another dressing.

2 heads iceberg lettuce, cleaned and cut into bite sized pieces
1 head romaine lettuce, cleaned and cut into bite sized pieces

1/4 cup carrot, shredded
1/4 cup red cabbage, shredded
8 ounces Genoa salami, thinly sliced and diced
8 ounces ham, thinly sliced and diced
4 ounces provolone cheese, shredded
4 ounces mozzarella cheese, shredded

Olive Salad
2/3 cup large green olives, pitted and coarsely chopped
2/3 cup medium green olives, pitted and coarsely chopped
1 (16 oz) jar Giardiniera
1/2 cup pimento, chopped
4 cloves garlic, minced
1 tablespoon capers, drained and rinsed
1/2 cup fresh parsley, finely-chopped
1 teaspoon fresh oregano, finely chopped
1 tablespoon red wine vinegar
3/4 cup extra virgin olive oil

In a medium bowl, combine all ingredients and then allow the flavors to blend for at least 2 hours prior to serving. Store, covered, in the refrigerator until ready to use.

Salad
Mix together lettuce, carrot and cabbage. Put the lettuce mixture into four chilled bowls. On top of each salad, put 2 ounces of salami, 2 ounces ham, 1 ounce provolone, 1 ounce mozzarella, and 3/4 cup olive salad. Feeds 4.

Oriental Chicken Salad

This salad is not your ordinary salad. Created at Cannon's restaurant, the Oriental chicken salad contains items not often seen in green salads. The Thai peanut vinaigrette is not a spicy dressing, as most people associate Thai food with heat. The chow mein noodles act as croutons for crunchiness.

2 cups green cabbage, shredded
5 cups romaine lettuce, shredded
1 cup green peas, thawed from frozen
1/2 cup carrots, grated
1/2 cup celery, chopped

3/4 cup bamboo shoots
Thai Peanut Vinaigrette (page 65)
4 (5 ounce) skinless chicken breast, grilled and cut into strips
Chow mein noodles

Mix cabbage, lettuce, peas, carrots, celery, and bamboo shoots in large bowl. Put into four chilled bowls. Put 3 ounces of the Thai peanut vinaigrette on top of salad. Place chicken on top of salad and cover with a handful of chow mein noodles. Feeds four.

Perry Street Pasta Salad

I have gotten many requests for this recipe. Perry Street was the street I on which I was living in Gretna, Louisiana, when Katrina hit. It is also where a lot of these recipes were developed. I was thinking of something to bring to a BBQ and thought of a pasta salad. So, I threw this together and was pleased with the results. I think that this is my only recipe that I did not tinker with as the first attempt was perfect.

24 ounces rainbow rotini, cooked al dente
2 tablespoons olive oil
Salt
1/2 large green bell pepper, diced
1/2 large yellow bell pepper, diced
1/2 large red bell pepper, diced
1 bunch green onions, sliced thin
1 pint grape tomatoes
1 can (2.25 ounce) black olives, sliced and drained
1 pound ham, diced
1 tablespoon Italian seasoning
1 tablespoon *Creole Seasoning Blend* (page 146)
1 tablespoon granulated garlic
16-ounce bottle Robusto Italian dressing

Cook pasta in water with olive oil and salt until al dente. Cool with running water. Add vegetables and ham to the pasta and toss. Add dry seasonings to salad and toss. Add salad dressing and toss. Refrigerate at least 2 hours before serving. Toss before serving

Uptown Salad

Here is another popular salad from Cannon's restaurant. It is a great summertime dish. You can make this dish even healthier by reducing the amount of cheese you use. It also makes a great quick dinner.

2 heads iceberg lettuce, cleaned and chopped
1 head romaine lettuce, cleaned and chopped

Mix lettuce together and keep cold.

1 1/2 cups Cheddar cheese, shredded
1 1/2 cups Monterey jack cheese, shredded

Mix the cheeses together and keep cold.

1 cup boiled egg, chopped
8 ounces ham, cubed
8 ounces smoked turkey, cubed
2 cups croutons
Green onion, chopped

To build your salads, place lettuce in four separate chilled bowls. Top with your favorite dressing. Then, place in order: croutons, cheese mixture, egg, ham, and turkey. Garnish with green onions and serve. Feeds four.

Warm Spinach Salad

This warm (or wilted) spinach salad is very versatile. You can serve this meatless, without the bacon bits on top. You can also serve this with a grilled chicken breast for a larger meal. Your options are endless.

Hot Bacon Dressing (page 65)
9-10 ounces baby spinach leaves, washed
1 cup fresh parsley leaves
1 cup croutons
1 cup boiled egg, diced
1/2 cup Parmesan cheese, shredded

Prepare hot bacon dressing. Mix spinach and parsley in a large bowl. Pour in dressing and mix well. Divide into four salad bowls. Top with croutons, eggs and Parmesan cheese. Serve immediately.

1000 Island Dressing

4 cups mayonnaise
3/4 cup celery, diced
1/2 cup onion, diced
3/4 cups boiled eggs, diced

1/2 cup sweet pickle relish
1 1/2 cups chili sauce
Pinch white pepper
1/8 teaspoon salt

Place mayonnaise in a large mixing bowl. Add all ingredients and mix well. Let the dressing sit for 5 hours before serving.

Bleu Cheese Dressing

4 cups mayonnaise
3/4-pound sour cream
1 tablespoon red wine vinegar
1/2 teaspoon Worcestershire sauce
1/2 teaspoon Crystal hot sauce
1/2 cup heavy cream
1/4 cup milk
1 1/2 teaspoons salt
1 1/2 teaspoons white pepper
2 tablespoons onion, minced
1 1/2 teaspoons green onions, minced
1 1/2 teaspoons garlic, minced
1 1/2 teaspoons fresh parsley, chopped
3/4-pound bleu cheese crumbles

Place mayonnaise and sour cream in a large mixing bowl. Mix in onion, green onion and garlic. Add all other ingredients except the bleu cheese and mix well. Add bleu cheese and mix thoroughly.

Caesar Dressing

2 eggs
1 tablespoon Worcestershire sauce
1 tablespoon lemon juice
6 tablespoons red wine vinegar
2 tablespoons garlic, chopped
2 (2 ounce) cans flat anchovy filets
1 tablespoon Dijon mustard
1 1/2 cups olive oil
1 teaspoon dry mustard
4 tablespoons Romano cheese, grated
1/4 teaspoon black pepper
1/4 teaspoon salt

In a blender, whip eggs. Add Worcestershire sauce, lemon juice, vinegar, and garlic, then blend. Add anchovies and Dijon mustard; blend. Blend in the olive oil very slowly. Add the remaining ingredients and blend. Refrigerate.

Honey Mustard Dressing

1/2 cup + 2 tablespoons vegetable oil
1/2 cup + 2 tablespoons honey
3 tablespoons yellow mustard
3 1/4 tablespoons cider vinegar
3/4 teaspoons onion salt
1/2 teaspoon cayenne pepper
4 cups mayonnaise

Mix all ingredients except mayo. Add mayo and mix until smooth in texture.

Refrigerate for an hour before serving.

Hot Bacon Dressing

2 ounces bacon, diced
1 tablespoon flour
2 tablespoons sugar
1 large egg, beaten
1/4 cup apple cider vinegar
1 cup water
Salt and pepper to taste

Fry bacon until crisp. Remove from pan. In a medium bowl, beat the other ingredients then add to the bacon drippings. Cook over low heat, stirring until thick, about 3-5 minutes. Season well with salt and pepper. Pour over salad and toss. Serve at once.

Thai Peanut Vinaigrette

3 cups *Vinaigrette Dressing* (page 66)
1/4 cup + 2 tablespoons sugar
3/4 cup creamy peanut butter
3/4 cup soy sauce
1 teaspoon crushed red pepper flakes

Mix until smooth.

CHEF TOMMY CENTOLA

Vinaigrette Dressing

1 cup olive oil
1 cup vegetable oil
3/4 cup salad vinegar
1/4 cup brown mustard
2 tablespoons sugar
1/4 teaspoon salt
3/4 teaspoon basil
3/4 teaspoon oregano
3/4 teaspoon thyme
3/4 teaspoon ground black pepper
1 tablespoon garlic, minced
1 1/2 teaspoon lemon juice

Mix all ingredients in a blender.

Seafood

New Orleans is blessed being surrounded by water. Louisiana is known as the Sportsman's Paradise. While hunting is popular, more people in Louisiana spend their sportsman's time harvesting the water. Many varieties of fish, shrimp, oysters, crabs, crawfish, alligator, frogs, and turtles live in the waters around New Orleans. Creoles and Cajuns alike have made use of this plentiful bounty in their cuisines.

With all the advances in freezing and shipping, seafood is available throughout the world. But there is nothing like cooking seafood hours after it has come from the water.

Alligator Sauce Piquant
BBQ Shrimp
BBQ Shrimp & Grits
Bronzed Grouper
Catfish Etienne
Catfish with Pecans
Crab Cakes
Crabmeat au Gratin
Crawfish Étouffée
Crawfish Pie
Creole Catfish
Fried Soft-Shell Crabs with Crabmeat
Frog Legs Abigail
Redfish Courtbouillon
Redfish Francis
Salmon Croquettes
Seafood Stuffed Mirlitons
Shrimp Creole
Stuffed Crab
Stuffed Eggplant Pirogue Peggy
Stuffed Shrimp
Stuffed Trout

Alligator Sauce Picante

This dish features the most menacing animal from the local water. Alligator meat does not taste like chicken. The best part to eat is the tail meat. You need to make sure that the meat is free of fat, which can lead to a gamy taste. Sauce Picante is a spicy tomato sauce. It is great with any meat, especially chicken.

2 pounds alligator tail meat, cubed
2 tablespoons *Seafood Seasoning Blend* (page 148)
1 cup vegetable oil
1 cup flour
2 cups onion, chopped
2 cups celery, chopped
2 cups green bell peppers, chopped
2 tablespoons garlic, chopped
1 29 ounce can tomato sauce
1 28 ounce can Rotel tomatoes
2 cups *Seafood Stock* (page 149) or *Chicken Stock* (page 146)
3 teaspoons dark brown sugar
3 bay leaves
2 teaspoons fresh thyme, chopped
2 teaspoons fresh oregano, chopped
3 teaspoons fresh basil, chopped
2 teaspoons salt
2 teaspoons cayenne pepper

Season the meat well with seafood seasoning blend. In a large pot, heat oil over low-medium heat. Brown meat in oil. Remove the meat and make a roux using the fat and flour, cooking it to a medium brown color. Add onion, celery and bell pepper. When the pot is somewhat cooled, add the garlic and sauté the vegetables over medium heat until tender. Add tomato sauce, Rotel, seafood stock and brown sugar. Cook for 3 minutes. Add the seasonings and simmer until thickened and meat is tender. Serve over hot rice.

BBQ Shrimp

This is one of my wife's favorite dishes. Every time we come back from New Orleans, we always have three pounds of large head-on shrimp to cook for dinner the night we get home. BBQ Shrimp is not shrimp that are cooked on a pit and covered with sauce. They are cooked in a highly seasoned, not spicy, combination of olive oil and butter. Make sure you have plenty of French bread to dip into the sauce. You can use headless shrimp, but you will not get the flavors that are released from the head.

1 1/2-pound butter (6 sticks)
1 1/2 cups olive oil

8 tablespoons garlic, chopped
2 tablespoons dried basil leaves
4 teaspoons salt
3 teaspoons lemon juice
2 tablespoons Worcestershire sauce
4 tablespoons ground black pepper
2 teaspoons dried oregano
2 teaspoons dried thyme
2 teaspoons BBQ seasoning
1 tablespoon *Creole Seasoning Blend* (page 146)
3 pounds 15-20 or larger shrimp head & tail on

Melt butter and olive oil in a large pot. Combine all other ingredients, adding shrimp last. Cook on stovetop on medium-high heat for 10 minutes. Serve in bowls with plenty of French bread to soak up the sauce.

BBQ Shrimp & Grits

Shrimp and grits is the state dish of South Carolina. In the Low country around Charleston, shrimp and grits is the traditional breakfast during shrimp season. It has since become a wonderful dish served all day long. The first time I tried this dish, I thought that it would be great using New Orleans style BBQ Shrimp. Try it next time, you will be glad you did.

BBQ Shrimp (See previous recipe)

Grits

3/4 cup quick grits
3 cups water
1/4 teaspoon salt
2 Tablespoons butter
2 cups shredded Cheddar cheese

In a medium saucepan, bring water to boil. Add the grits and salt. Stir well with a whisk. Reduce heat to medium-low. Cover. Cook for 5 minutes or until thickened. Remove from heat and stir in the butter and cheese. Keep covered until ready to serve.

Put grits in 4 bowls. Place shrimp on top with a little of shrimp sauce.

Bronzed Grouper

Bronzing is a cooking method close to blackening. The fish is seasoned the same way. The cooking method is different. Blackening requires a white-hot cast iron skillet to quickly cook the fish to form a well-seasoned crust. This method creates a lot of smoke. At home, most cooks prepare a blackened dish outdoors. When you bronze a dish, you use a pan that is not as hot. You are basically sautéing the fish over high heat. You still get a great seasoning crust when you bronze a dish.

4 (8-ounce) grouper fillets
1 stick butter, melted
Blackening Seasoning (page 144)

Heat a large sauté pan over medium heat. Dip grouper in butter. Season both sides with plenty of blackening seasoning. Cook evenly on both sides until fish is flaky. You can serve this with a little bit of melted butter on the side for dipping.

Catfish Étienne

Catfish is very popular here in Arkansas. This dish from Cannon's restaurant fits in well here. With crawfish tails available in most groceries, you will not have a problem finding all the ingredients needed for preparation. Although there are three separate recipes used in this dish, it is a very easy dish to recreate. I make a big batch of seafood breading and keep it in an airtight container to use, as I need it.

Cream of Crawfish Sauce (page 107)
4 (6-ounce) catfish fillets
Egg Wash (page 147)
Seafood Breading (page 148)
Fresh parsley, chopped

Preheat deep fryer to 350°F. Prepare crawfish sauce and keep it warm. Dip catfish into egg wash, then coat with seafood breading. Shake off the excess breading and fry for 5 minutes or until fish is done. Drain on paper towels and place one fillet on each serving plate. Top with crawfish sauce and sprinkle with parsley.

Catfish with Pecans

One day at Commander's Palace restaurant, Ella Brennan wanted a dish to replace Trout Almandine using local ingredients. The dish that was created was trout with pecans. Since trout is not common in Arkansas, I make it with catfish. The combination is fantastic. This is a favorite during pecan season.

4, 5 to 7 ounce, catfish fillets
Creole Seafood Seasoning (page 146)
Egg Wash (page 147)
Seafood Breading (page 148)

Canola oil for cooking catfish
Meunière sauce (page 109)
1/3 cup pecans, coarsely chopped

While making meunière sauce, add pecans to sauce so the pecans can brown with the butter. Rinse fillets and pat dry. Season both sides with seafood seasoning. Dip each fillet in egg wash, and then dredge in seafood breading, shaking off excess. Generously coat the bottom of a large skillet with oil and heat over moderately high heat. Sauté fillets, turning once, until golden brown and crisp, 3-4 minutes on each side. Place fillet on serving plate and top with pecan meunière sauce.

Crab Cakes

This recipe made me think about writing a cookbook. I had entered it for the Thomas Kinkade cookbook contest. Three recipes were selected from his fans to be included in his wife's cookbook. I was told that two of my recipes were selected. Since they wanted three different people included in the book, only my crab cakes were chosen. They would not tell me which of my other recipes won. This recipe was also published in the June 2009 edition of *Louisiana Cookin'* magazine. So here is my award-winning recipe.

1 pound crabmeat
1 tablespoon butter
4 cloves garlic, chopped
1/3 cup green onion, chopped
1/4 cup fresh parsley, chopped
1 tablespoon Old Bay Seafood seasoning
3/4 cup heavy cream
3/4 cup seasoned breadcrumbs
1/4 teaspoon salt
1/4 teaspoon black pepper
1/4 teaspoon fresh basil leaves, chopped

Pick through crabmeat, removing pieces of shells. Set aside. Over medium heat, melt butter in a medium saucepan. Sauté garlic in butter until golden brown. Add green onion and cook until soft. Add parsley and cook 1 minute. Add crabmeat to pan. Add Old Bay seasoning and mix thoroughly. Add heavy cream and mix well. Add breadcrumbs and mix well. The mixture should not be liquidly; if so, add more breadcrumbs. Add salt, pepper, and basil; mix well. Allow mixture to cool. Form cakes in hand, making a 2 1/2-inch circle. Place on a foil-lined cookie sheet. Refrigerate for at least two hours. Cook in a 350°F oven for 10 minutes. You may also deep fry them by heating a fryer to 360°F. Dip crab cake in mixture of milk and beaten egg, then cover with breadcrumbs. Cook them for 3 minutes or until golden brown.

Crabmeat au Gratin

This dish is a delightful way to showcase lump crabmeat. It can be served as a casserole or in individual portion dishes. It is also an easy dish to experiment with; you can change up the cheeses to get a different flavor. Just make sure you let your diners know about the change. I know a man who had ordered Crabmeat au Gratin in a restaurant. He was very surprised and disappointed that the dish was made with smoked Gouda cheese.

2 egg yolks
12 ounces heavy cream
1/2 stick butter (4 ounces)
1 large onion, minced
3 cloves garlic, minced
1 teaspoon salt
1/2 teaspoon white pepper
1 tablespoon *Seafood Seasoning Blend* (page 148)
1/4 cup flour
1/2 cup shredded mild cheddar cheese
1/2 cup shredded Monterey jack cheese
1 pound lump crabmeat, picked through for shells
1 cup seasoned bread crumbs
1 cup shredded sharp cheddar cheese

Preheat oven to 400°F. Lightly grease a 9x9-inch baking dish. In a bowl, whip together egg yolks and heavy cream. Melt butter in a large saucepan over medium heat. Sauté onions and garlic about 3 minutes. Season with salt, white pepper and the seafood seasoning blend. Reduce heat to low, cover, and simmer 20 minutes, stirring occasionally, until very tender. Mix the flour into the saucepan, and cook for 5 minutes, stirring continuously. Mix in egg yolk mixture. Stir in the mild cheddar and Monterey jack cheeses until melted. Remove from heat and fold in crabmeat. Transfer the mixture to the prepared baking dish. Top with breadcrumbs and sharp cheddar cheese. Bake 20 minutes until bubbling lightly.

Crawfish Étouffée

In French, étouffée means smothered, which means that this dish has many variations. The biggest decision is whether or not to include tomatoes. With this version, I chose not to use them. To me, a dish that is smothered is one cooked with lots of butter and onions. Either way you cook it, you will be eating a Louisiana favorite.

1 pound crawfish tails
1 tablespoon *Seafood Seasoning Blend* (page 148)
4 tablespoons butter
1 medium onion, minced
3 cloves garlic, minced
1/2 cup green bell pepper, minced
1/2 cup water
1/4 cup green onion, chopped
1/4 cup fresh parsley, chopped
Cooked rice

Season crawfish with seafood seasoning blend. Melt butter and add the onion, garlic and bell pepper, stirring constantly, and cook until wilted. Add water and bring to a boil. Reduce heat and simmer for 15-20 minutes. Add green onion and parsley and simmer 5 minutes more. Serve over hot rice.

Crawfish Pie

Hank Williams sang the words "jambalaya, crawfish pie, filé gumbo", in his song "Jambalaya on the Bayou." This is a popular way to eat crawfish that have already been cooked and peeled. When using frozen crawfish tails, make sure they are from the U.S. While the imported crawfish are okay, they do not have the same flavor.

1 (9-inch) prepared deep-dish pie crust
1/4 cup butter
1 cup onion, chopped
1/2 cup green bell pepper, chopped
1/2 cup celery, chopped
1 teaspoon *Creole Seasoning Blend* (page 146)
1/4 teaspoon ground black pepper
1/4 teaspoon cayenne pepper
1/8 teaspoon white pepper
1 cup diced tomato
1 pound peeled crawfish tails
2 tablespoons flour
1 Cup *Seafood Stock* (page 149) or *Chicken Stock* (page 146)

Place the pie crust into a deep-dish pie plate. Melt butter in a large skillet over medium heat, and cook the onions, bell pepper, celery, and dry seasonings, stirring occasionally, until the vegetables are tender and the onion is translucent, about 5 minutes. Stir in the tomato and crawfish tails, reduce the heat to medium-low, and cook for 3 minutes to marry the flavors, stirring occasionally. Whisk flour and stock together in a bowl until the mixture is smooth. Pour the flour mixture into the crawfish mixture. Bring the filling to a simmer.

Cook, stirring constantly, until the mixture thickens, about 5 minutes. Remove from heat and allow to stand for 20 to 30 minutes to finish thickening. While filling is cooling, preheat oven to 400°F. Pour the filling into the piecrust, and bake until the crust is golden brown and the filling is hot, 30 to 40 minutes. Cool for 10 minutes before serving.

Creole Catfish

This dish I created as a Friday lunch special at Cannon's restaurant. We were looking for something that was not as heavy as the catfish Étienne. I had seen other restaurants topping their fish with crawfish étouffée. I thought I would try fried catfish topped with shrimp Creole. The dish was a success. It became so popular that we continued it as an all-day Friday special.

4 (5-to-7-ounce) catfish fillets
Egg Wash (page 147)
Seafood Breading (page 148)
Shrimp Creole (page 78)
Fresh parsley, chopped

Heat deep fryer to 375°F. Dip catfish in egg wash, shaking off excess. Dredge the catfish in the seafood breading, shaking off the excess. Fry for 3-5 minutes or until the fish float to the surface of the fryer. Top with hot shrimp Creole and garnish with parsley.

Fried Soft-Shell Crab with Crabmeat

This is my rendition of a popular dish from LeRuth's restaurant. It is the ultimate in crab dishes. First, start with a delicate fried soft-shell crab. Then, you top it with crabmeat that has been heated up in a meunière sauce. This is the first entrée that I ate at LeRuth's. It was everything that I expected and more. I found out that the chef had put almost a pound of crabmeat on top (the benefits of working there).

How to select and clean Soft Shell Crabs

When buying soft-shell crabs, fresh ones are the best but they are not always easy to find. To select the tastiest, use your nose. When fresh, they smell clean and astringent, like sea mist, a fitting aroma for a delicacy that both captures the romance of the sea and the allure of a full moon in spring.

1. To clean soft-shell crabs, hold the crab in one hand, and using a pair of kitchen shears, cut off the front of the crab, about 1/2 inch behind the eyes and mouth. Squeeze out the contents of the sack located directly behind the cut you just made.

2. Lift one pointed end of the crab's outer shell; remove and discard the gills. Repeat on the other side.

3. Turn the crab over and snip off the small flap known as the apron. Rinse the entire crab well and pat dry. Once cleaned, crabs should be cooked or frozen immediately.

Meunière Sauce (page 109)
1 pound lump crabmeat, picked through to remove loose shells.
4 soft shell crabs
Egg Wash (page 147)
Seafood Breading (page 148)
Fresh parsley, chopped

Preheat deep fryer to 350°F. Make meunière sauce and add the crabmeat. Cook for 2 minutes then keep warm. Dip cleaned crabs in egg wash, shaking off excess. Then dredge seafood breading, shaking off excess. Fry for 3-5 minutes or until done. Drain on paper towels. Top each crab with 1/4 of the crabmeat mixture. Sprinkle parsley on top and serve.

Frog Legs Abigail

I have always loved frog legs. It seems that my dog, Abigail, likes them, too. She is always searching the yard looking for frogs. When she finds them, she chases them and tries to bite them. So, I lovingly name this dish after my little girl.

16 pair frog legs, separated
1 teaspoon salt
1/2 teaspoon white pepper
1 tablespoon *Seafood Seasoning Blend* (page 148)
1 cup flour
1/2 cup olive oil
2 teaspoons garlic, minced
2 tablespoons clam juice
1 tablespoon lemon juice
1 tablespoon heavy cream
6 tablespoons butter, cold, cut into 1-tablespoon pieces
1 tablespoon fresh parsley, chopped
Pinch black pepper

Lightly season legs with 1/2 teaspoon salt and 1/4 teaspoon white pepper. Combine flour with seafood seasoning blend and the remaining salt and pepper. In batches, dredge legs in flour and shake off the excess. Heat olive oil in a large sauté pan over medium-high heat. Add legs in two batches and cook, turning constantly until golden brown 2 to 3 minutes per side. Drain on paper towels. Carefully drain all but 1 tablespoon of oil from the pan and return to heat. Add garlic and cook, stirring, until fragrant, about 30 seconds. Add clam and lemon juices and bring to a boil. Cook until reduces by half, about 1 minute. Add heavy cream and cook for 30 seconds. Reduce heat to medium-low and add the butter, several pieces at a time, stirring constantly, until all the butter has been incorporated. Remove from heat. Stir in parsley and black pepper. Return legs to pan and cook over medium heat to warm through, shaking pan back and forth to coat evenly with sauce, about 1 minute.

Redfish Courtbouillon

I have been told that my father-in-law was a great cook. I keep hearing about him cooking Redfish Courtbouillon. No one knows what happened to the recipe. So, to honor Wesley Anderson, here is a recipe for Redfish Courtbouillon.

1/4 cup butter
1/4 cup flour
2 teaspoons green onion, chopped
2 cups onion, finely chopped
1/2 cup celery, finely chopped
1 green bell pepper, finely chopped
1 large can tomatoes, drained reserving the liquid
3 cloves garlic, minced
2 bay leaves
1/2 teaspoon marjoram
1/4 teaspoon basil
Salt and pepper to taste
1/4 teaspoon thyme
1 teaspoon Crystal hot sauce
1 teaspoon Worcestershire sauce
2 cups *Seafood Stock* (page 149)
2 1/2 pounds redfish fillets, cut into chunks, 2-3 inches wide
Hot cooked rice

In a heavy pot on medium-low, heat butter. Add flour and cook for 10 minutes or golden brown, stirring constantly. Reduce the heat and stir in the onions, celery and bell pepper. Cook until the vegetables are soft, stirring often. Add the tomatoes and cook five minutes. Stir in dry seasonings, Worcestershire sauce and hot sauce. Slowly stir in one cup of the reserved tomato liquid and stock. Simmer for five minutes. Add redfish and adjust seasonings. Cover and simmer about 30 minutes or until the fish is cooked. Serve over hot rice.

Redfish Francis

My mother's middle name was Francis. This dish is exquisite and full of flavor. In New Orleans, this dish would be called Redfish Pontchartrain. Most dishes topped with any type of crab are named after the large lake that borders New Orleans to the North. However, I chose to honor my mother with the name.

Meunière Sauce (page 109)
1 pound lump crabmeat, picked through to remove loose shells.
4 8-ounce redfish fillets
1 stick butter, melted
Blackening Seasoning (page 144)
Fresh parsley, chopped

Make meunière sauce and add the crabmeat. Cook for 2 minutes then keep warm. Heat a large sauté pan over medium heat. Dip redfish in butter. Season both sides with plenty of blackening seasoning. Cook evenly on both sides until fish is flaky. Place on serving plate and add 1/4 of the crabmeat sauce. Top with parsley and serve.

Salmon Croquettes

This recipe brings back memories of my youth. My mother would make these occasionally on Friday nights. The crunchiness of the outside was a perfect counter balance to the soft inside. Every time I heard that we were having salmon croquettes for dinner, I would be the first one at the table. I can almost taste them now. This is how my mother wrote down the recipe.

Fry:
1 tablespoon minced onion
3 tablespoons margarine or butter

Blend in:
1/3 cup flour

Add:
1 cup of milk
1 well-beaten egg
Cook to thicken

Add:
1 teaspoon salt
1 tablespoon lemon juice
2 tablespoons sherry
1 can salmon

Allow to cool.

Form croquettes; roll them in breadcrumbs. Roll in beaten egg mixed with a little water. Roll again in breadcrumbs. Refrigerate. Fry in deep fat fryer at 365°F.

Seafood Stuffed Mirliton

People outside of Louisiana know mirliton as chayote squash or vegetable pear. The mirliton is a member of the same family as melons, cucumbers and squash. It is perfect for stuffing. Here is a recipe that is sure to please.

8 medium mirlitons
1 3/4 cups onion, minced
1/3 cup fresh parsley, minced
1/3 cup green bell pepper, minced
3 cloves garlic, minced
1 teaspoon fresh thyme, minced
2 bay leaves
1 1/2 pounds shrimp peeled, deveined and diced
1/4-pound ham, diced
1/2-pound crabmeat
1 tablespoon *Creole Seasoning Blend* (page 146)
2 eggs, beaten
2 sticks butter
2 cups seasoned bread crumbs

Preheat oven to 350°F. Place the mirlitons in a large saucepan. Cover with water, bring it to a boil and cook for 15 minutes. Remove the mirlitons to a platter and cool until they are easy to handle. Halve the mirlitons, and then remove the pit and scoop out all of the meat, reserving the shells. Dice the meat and set aside. Sauté onion, parsley, bell pepper, garlic, thyme and bay leaves in butter for 10 minutes. Next add shrimp, ham, crabmeat, Creole seasoning, and mirliton meat. Mix and sauté gently for 30 minutes. Remove from heat, and vigorously stir in beaten eggs. Add enough breadcrumbs to bind. Divide the stuffing between mirliton halves; sprinkle the remaining breadcrumbs on top and dot with butter. Bake until the crust is golden brown about 15 minutes.

Shrimp Creole

Shrimp Creole is a dish that most tourists try when they come to New Orleans. It is not a very spicy dish like most people think all New Orleans foods are. It does show the Creole influence with the inclusion of tomatoes in the dish. This dish is mostly served on rice, but it also makes a great sauce on fish.

1 tablespoon canola oil
1 medium onion, chopped
1 cup celery, chopped
1/4 cup green onion, chopped
1 small green bell pepper, thinly sliced

3 cloves garlic, minced
1 dash cayenne pepper
1 dash dried thyme
1 teaspoon *Creole Seasoning Blend* (page 146)
2 bay leaves
1 can (14.5 ounce) whole peeled tomatoes, drained and crushed
3 ounces tomato paste
3 pounds medium shrimp, peeled and deveined
Cooked rice

Heat oil in a heavy skillet over medium heat. Sauté onion, celery, green onion, bell pepper, garlic, thyme, cayenne, Creole seasoning, and bay leaves for a few minutes, until the vegetables are tender. Add tomatoes and tomato paste and simmer for 15 minutes. Add shrimp and simmer for 10 minutes. Remove bay leaves. Serve over cooked rice.

Stuffed Crab

Stuffed crabs have been put on the endangered recipe list. I myself am as guilty as the rest. Stuffed crab was a common fixture on fried seafood platters around the Gulf Coast. But since crab cakes have less of a bread component, and the stuffed crab has almost fifty-percent breading, crab cakes are considered gourmet. The stuffed crab is still a great dish. My Aunt Shirley would make dozens of them for a local festival. It is also versatile. This dish can be used as stuffing for other seafood dishes. I also like using claw meat in stuffed crabs. It gives you a stronger crab flavor.

1 stick butter
1/2 cup onion, minced
1/2 cup celery, minced
1/4 cup green onion, sliced
1/4 cup fresh parsley, chopped
1 pound claw crabmeat, picked through for shells
1 1/2 cups seasoned bread crumbs
1/2 teaspoon *Seafood Seasoning Blend* (page 148)

Preheat oven to 375°F. Melt butter in medium sauté pan over medium heat. Add onion, celery, green onion, and parsley and cook until soft, about 3 minutes. Add crabmeat and remove from heat. Add breadcrumbs and seafood seasoning and mix well. You can either scoop into real crab shells, individual serving dishes, or in a 9x9-buttered pan. Bake for 15 to 20 minutes.

Stuffed Eggplant Pirogue Peggy

My wife Peggy loves eggplant. Every couple of months, we drive over an hour to Copeland's in West Little Rock. Her main reason to go there is one dish, Eggplant Pirogue. A pirogue is a flat bottom boat that is used in the swamps of Louisiana. This dish resembles a pirogue, half of the eggplant stuffed with plenty of seafood.

3 medium eggplants, cut in half lengthwise
1 tablespoon olive oil
1/2 cup ham, diced small
1/2 cup onion, chopped
1/4 cup yellow bell pepper, chopped
3 cloves garlic, chopped
1/2 cup *Seafood Stock* (page 149)
1/2 pound medium shrimp, peeled, deveined and chopped
1/2 pound lump crabmeat, cleaned of shells
1/2 cup seasoned bread crumbs
6 tablespoons fresh Parmesan cheese, grated and divided
1/4 cup green onions, finely chopped
1 tablespoon fresh basil, chopped
1 1/2 teaspoons fresh tarragon, chopped
1 teaspoon lemon zest
1 1/2 teaspoon *Creole Seasoning Blend* (page 146)

Preheat oven to 425°F. Score cut side of each eggplant half in a crisscross pattern. Lightly coat cut sides of eggplant with cooking spray. Place eggplant halves, cut side down, on a baking sheet. Bake for 10 minutes. Turn the eggplant halves over and bake for an additional 10 minutes or until tender. Remove from oven and let cool for 10 minutes. Remove pulp for the eggplant, leaving a 1/4-inch-thick shell. Place eggplant shells on baking sheet coated with cooking spray. Chop pulp and put aside. Reduce oven to 350°F. Heat olive oil in a large nonstick skillet over medium-high heat. Add ham, onion, bell pepper, and garlic. Sauté for 5 minutes.

Add reserved eggplant pulp and stock, cooking for 10 minutes or until most of the liquid evaporates, stirring occasionally. Stir in shrimp and crabmeat, cook 1 minute and remove from heat. Add breadcrumbs, three tablespoons Parmesan cheese, green onions, basil, tarragon, lemon zest, and Creole seasoning, stirring gently to combine. Mound about 1/2 cup of seafood mixture into each shell. Sprinkle each with the remaining Parmesan cheese. Bake for 15 minutes or until thoroughly heated and shrimp are done.

Stuffed Shrimp

Just by looking at the name of the dish, one may wonder, how can you put stuffing in a shrimp? The answer to that question is to put the stuffing around the shrimp. The key to this dish is to make sure the stuffing (Stuffed Crab recipe) has cooled enough to stay firm around the shrimp. If not, you will have stuffing floating in the oil.

24 medium-to-large shrimp, peeled and deveined but tail-on
Stuffed Crab (page 79)
2 tablespoons *Seafood Seasoning Blend* (page 148)
Egg Wash (page 147)
Seafood Breading (page 148)

Make the stuffed crab recipe. Allow it to completely cool. Season shrimp with seafood seasoning blend. Wrap each shrimp with about 1/3 cup of stuffed crab. Allow to set in refrigerator for at least an hour. Heat deep fryer to 350 degrees. Dip shrimp in egg wash, shaking off the excess. Dredge the shrimp in the seafood breading, shaking off the excess. Fry for about 4-5 minutes. Drain on paper towel. Serve with Remoulade or Hollandaise sauce for dipping.

Stuffed Trout

This dish is a recreation of the Stuffed Trout that LeRuth's restaurant used to serve. The trout used here is the speckled trout, a salt-water fish, found in the Gulf of Mexico; not the fresh-water rainbow trout. If you cannot find trout, catfish makes a great substitution.

4 (5–7-ounce) trout fillets
Stuffed Crab (page 79)
Seafood Seasoning Blend (page 148)
4 tablespoons melted butter
Hollandaise Sauce (page 108)
Fresh parsley, chopped

Preheat oven to 350°F. Butter a 9x9-inch baking dish. Wash trout and pat dry. Sprinkle both sides with seafood seasoning. Put a 1/2 cup of stuffed crab on top of the trout. Roll the trout up and secure it with a toothpick. Place trout in baking pan and spoon 1 tablespoon of melted butter over the fillet. Bake for 30 minutes. After putting trout on serving plate, spoon Hollandaise sauce over trout. Garnish with fresh parsley.

Meats

New Orleanians do not live on seafood alone. Chicken has always been a mainstay in New Orleans restaurants. Beef has never been a big player in New Orleans. Beef was not raised in Louisiana. So, seafood, chicken and pork became the most used proteins in New Orleans. When the Italians arrived, veal started to become popular. When you are looking for a non-seafood New Orleans dish, the following recipes will be sure to please.

Boudin Stuffed Pork Chops
Bruccoloni
Bruno's Cajun Meatloaf
Cajun Fried Turkey
Chicken Bonne Femme
Chicken Cacciatore
Chicken Clemenceau
Chicken Delight
Chicken Florentine
Chicken Grande
Chicken Marsala
Chicken Oregano
Chicken Pontalb
Fried Chicken
Leg of Lamb
Osso Buco
Panéed Veal
Pork Chops and Artichoke
Turkey Poulet
Veal Andrew
Veal Marie
Veal Parmesan
Veal Piccata
Veal Saltimbocca

Boudin Stuffed Pork Chops

While grocery shopping one day, I found some double-cut pork chops that I thought would be great for stuffing. I then started asking myself, *What kind of stuffing are you going to make?* Then, I saw some boudin in the sausage area. The light bulb in my head came on. Here is the result. If you wish, you can use some Bourbon Glaze (See Lagniappe for recipe) to give it another layer of flavor.

4 pork chops center cut 1½ inch thick
1 package boudin sausage casing removed
Creole Seasoning Blend (page 146)
Bourbon Glaze (optional) (page 144)

Preheat oven to 425°F. Cut pockets in the pork chops and stuff with Boudin. Secure the pocket with toothpicks. Sprinkle both sides of the chop with Creole seasoning. Cook pork chops for 25 minutes.

Bruccoloni

When most people think about New Orleans cuisine, Italian is not what comes to mind first. In the late 1800s, large number of immigrants from Sicily began to settle in South Louisiana. The Sicilians and the Creoles started combining their cuisines. There are many fantastic Italian restaurants in New Orleans. You can find some of the best meals in these restaurants. Bruccoloni can be made with either beef of veal. Not often will you find it on a restaurant menu. But I guarantee if you do find a restaurant that serves this dish, you will have one of your best Italian meals.

2 beef top round steaks, 1/4 inch thick
1 cup Italian flavored bread crumbs
2 eggs, slightly beaten
4 large garlic cloves, minced
1/2 cup Parmesan cheese, grated
1 medium onion, finely diced
2 hard-boiled eggs, chopped
Creole Seasoning Blend (page 146)
½ cup olive oil
Italian Red Sauce (page 109)
Cooked pasta
Grated Parmesan cheese

Place steaks on a cutting board, and trim fat from edges. Pound steaks to 1/8 inch thick, taking care not to tear. Preheat oven to 375°F. In a medium bowl, combine breadcrumbs, beaten eggs, garlic and cheese. Spread mixture over steaks, leaving a 1-inch border along the edges. Scatter the onions and boiled eggs over breadcrumb mixture. Beginning at long edges, roll tightly, like a jellyroll. Tie securely with butcher's string. Sprinkle Creole seasoning over rolls. Heat olive oil in a heavy skillet 12-inch skillet over medium heat. Add steak rolls, one at a time and brown on both sides. Place browned rolls in a 13x9-inch baking dish. Pour Italian red sauce over top of meat rolls. Bake in preheated oven until the meat is fork tender, about 45 minutes. To serve, remove string and slice 1/2-inch-thick slices. Serve with pasta topped with meat and sauce and garnished with Parmesan cheese.

Bruno's Cajun Meatloaf

Bruno was the first pet I ever had. He was my wife's pet when we met. He was our beloved Yorkie that lived to be eighteen. His favorite meal would be my leftover meatloaf. To be honest with you, I would make it large so he could enjoy it for days. This meatloaf will leave people barking for more.

2 1/2 pounds ground chuck (80 percent meat/20 percent fat)
1/3 cup onion, minced
1/3 cup garlic, minced
1/4 cup celery, minced
1/4 cup green bell pepper, minced
2 tablespoons Italian seasoning
1/4 cup *Creole Seasoning Blend* (page 146)
1/2 cup ketchup
1/4 cup Worcestershire sauce
2 large eggs
1 1/2 cups seasoned bread crumbs
Hot sauce to taste (optional)

Preheat oven to 400°F. Mix meat, onion, garlic, celery, bell pepper, and dry seasonings. Add ketchup and Worcestershire sauce and mix. Add eggs and breadcrumbs. Mix and shape into a loaf. Place onto a sheet pan covered with aluminum foil. Cook for 45 minutes. Allow to rest for 5 minutes before serving.

Cajun Fried Turkey

Cajun fried turkey is a delicious way to prepare your holiday main dish. It is not really a recipe, but a cooking technique. This dish can be very dangerous. If your bird is not dry when it goes in the fryer, there is a great chance of oil overflowing and possibly catching on fire. This is definitely something that cannot be done in a kitchen. When setting up your cooking pot (the same type of pot for boiled crawfish) make sure you have plenty of space around the pot, in case something goes wrong.

Turkey, up to 16 pounds cleaned and dry, giblets and neck removed
Peanut oil
A thermometer attached to the pot with the tip sticking in the oil

Creole Seasoning Blend (page 146)
Marinade and injector

Light the fryer and set at a low flame. Pour in peanut oil. (For a 10- to 12-pound turkey, use 1 1/2 to 2 gallons oil. For a 13- to 16-pound turkey use 2 1/2 to 3 gallons of oil.) Remember; do not over fill the pot. Heat oil to 325°F. Rub turkey with Creole seasoning. If you use a marinade, inject the turkey twice in each breast and once in the thigh. It will take 15-20 minutes per pound. Remember; use caution when frying a turkey. There are many ways you can burn yourself frying a turkey, but the flavor of the turkey makes it would the risk.

Chicken Bonne Femme

Chicken Bonne Femme is a dish that you will find on the menus of the older French Quarter restaurants. Bonne Femme translates to Good Woman, or Good Wife. But in French culinary terms it generally means with mushrooms. Many Creole restaurants, however, serve it without mushrooms, which is the way this recipe is prepared.

4 chicken breasts, boneless and skinless, pounded lightly for even cooking
Creole Seasoning Blend, to taste (page 146)
Salt and pepper, to taste
1/4 cup olive oil
3 tablespoons butter, divided
3 medium baking potatoes, peeled and sliced on 1/8-inch rounds
3/4 cup onion, diced
1/8 cup green onion, minced
1 cup ham, diced
2 cloves garlic, minced
1/4 cup white wine
1 tablespoon fresh parsley, minced

Preheat oven to 350°F. Season the chicken with Creole seasoning, salt and pepper. In a large sauté pan over medium high heat, add olive oil and 1 tablespoon of butter. When hot, add the chicken and sauté until golden brown on both sides. Remove from pan and set aside. Add the potatoes to the hot pan and sauté until tender. Add onions, ham and garlic. Cook until onions are translucent, occasionally stirring gently as to not break up the potatoes. Deglaze the pan with the white wine and cook for 2 minutes. Place the chicken breast back into the pan and cook in the oven until the chicken is done. Remove from oven; place the chicken on serving dishes. Add parsley and the remaining butter to the sauce, shaking the pan to incorporate. Spoon sauce over chicken and serve.

Chicken Cacciatore

Cacciatore is translated as the hunter's way. This dish is an easy one to prepare so that hunters would be able to eat a delicious and quick meal. Because it is a quick meal, this dish is very popular in fire stations. So, if you are looking for a quick Italian meal, give this a try.

1 1/2 pounds chicken breast boneless, skinless and cut into ½ inch strips
1 medium onion, julienned
1 medium green bell pepper, julienned
2 cloves garlic, chopped
2 tablespoons canola oil
1 (15-ounce) can tomato sauce
1 (14.5-ounce) can stewed tomatoes
1/2 teaspoon fresh oregano, chopped
1 teaspoon *Creole Seasoning Blend* (page 146)
Hot cooked rice

In a large skillet over medium heat, cook the chicken, onion, bell pepper, and garlic in oil until chicken is lightly browned on both sides and vegetables are tender. Add the tomato sauce, stewed tomatoes and seasonings; bring to a boil. Reduce heat and simmer, uncovered for 5 minutes or until heated through. Serve over rice.

Chicken Clemenceau

This dish was named for Georges Clemenceau, who was the French prime minister in 1906. A lot of restaurants in the French Quarter serve this dish, but it is unknown where it was created. You can use whole chicken for this dish or chicken breast, like I have.

Brabant Potatoes (page 113)
2 tablespoons olive oil
4 tablespoons butter, divided
4 chicken breasts, lightly pounded
2 cups mushrooms, thickly sliced
1 small onion, chopped
1 bunch green onions, chopped
3 cloves garlic, minced
1/2 cup dry white wine
Creole Seasoning Blend (page 146)
1 tablespoon fresh parsley, minced
1 cup small fresh green peas

Cook Brabant potatoes. When they are almost golden brown, heat olive oil and 2 tablespoons butter in an ovenproof skillet. When the oil is bubbling and hot, add the chicken; brown quickly on both sides and remove to a plate. In the same hot pan, add the mushrooms. Sauté them until they are golden brown. Add the onions and garlic, season with a little Creole seasoning. Sauté them until the onions are almost tender and have some color. Deglaze the pan with wine and cook for 2 minutes. Stir in 1 tablespoon parsley. Place the chicken back in the pan and cover with some of the sauce. Place in the oven until the chicken is cooked through. Warm the peas over low heat. Place potatoes on serving dishes making a pile in the center. Place a chicken breast on each pile. Melt the remaining butter into the sauce and fold in the peas. Spoon sauce over chicken and garnish with remaining parsley.

Chicken Delight

This is another one of my mother's recipes. Chicken delight is an easy dish to assemble. It is great on those nights when you want a home cooked meal but do not have a lot of time to prepare it. This dish also travels well. It is a great main dish for any occasion.

4 chicken breasts, cooked and diced
1 can cream of chicken soup
8 ounces sour cream
1 tube Ritz crackers, crushed
3/4 stick margarine, melted
Poppy seeds

Preheat oven to 350°F. Mix diced chicken, soup and sour cream together. Place the mixture in a greased baking dish. Mix crackers and margarine together. Put on top of the other mixture. Sprinkle poppy seeds on top of dish. Bake for 20-30 minutes.

Chicken Florentine

Any dish called Florentine is a dish served with spinach. If you have any leftover spinach dip, it can be used to make this dish. This classic Italian dish can also be made with other meats, like veal. It is rumored that this dish was a favorite of Popeye.

1 cup flour
Creole Seasoning Blend (page 146)
4 (6-ounce) chicken breasts, boneless and skinless
Egg Wash (page 147)
Olive oil
4 cloves garlic, minced, divided
1 cup white wine

1 tablespoon lemon juice
2 pounds fresh spinach, washed drained and chopped
4 tablespoons fresh parsley, minced
Hollandaise Sauce (page 108)

Season flour with Creole seasoning. Dredge the chicken breasts in the flour, then the egg wash, and then in the flour again. Heat a sauté pan over medium-high heat, then add enough olive oil to cover the bottom of the pan. Add 2 tablespoons of garlic and sauté for 1 minute, being careful not to burn the garlic. Add chicken breast and cook for about 2 minutes per side, or until they begin to turn white around the edges. Remove from pan and reserve on a plate, covering them with aluminum foil. Raise the heat to high. Add white wine and lemon juice to the pan, stirring with a wooden spoon to get up any bits of chicken on the bottom of the pan. Boil for 2-3 minutes to evaporate the alcohol, reducing the liquid by 20 percent. Turn off the heat and return the chicken to the pan. Cover to keep warm. Heat another sauté pan over medium-high heat. Add enough olive oil to cover the bottom of the pan. Add remaining 2 tablespoons of garlic and sauté for 1 minute. Add spinach, season with Creole seasoning, and sauté until wilted and thoroughly heated through. Place a mound of spinach on a serving plate. Place a breast on the pile and spoon some of the wine sauce on top. Top with a small stream of Hollandaise sauce and garnish with parsley.

Chicken Grande

Chicken grande is a delightful dish, which was created by Mosca's restaurant. Mosca's is located 20 minutes from the French Quarter on the Westbank of New Orleans in Westwego. It is easy to miss. It is a white shack with not much around it. But it serves some of the best Creole Italian food in the city. It is not a dish I would recommend on a date unless both people are eating it. This dish is a garlic lover's dream.

3/4 cup olive oil
1 (3-pound) chicken, cut into 8 pieces
2 teaspoons *Creole Seasoning Blend* (page 146)
6-10 cloves of garlic, unpeeled and mashed
1 teaspoon fresh rosemary leaves
1 teaspoon fresh oregano, chopped
½ cup *Chicken Stock* (page 146)

Heat olive oil over medium heat in a large skillet until hot. Add the chicken pieces, turning often. Cook the chicken until browned. Sprinkle chicken with Creole seasoning. Add garlic, rosemary, and oregano, stirring to distribute. Pour the chicken stock or broth over the chicken and simmer until the liquid has reduced by half. Serve chicken hot with pan juices.

Chicken Marsala

This dish is made with Marsala wine, which is produced on the island of Sicily. It is similar to Port wine, which is usually served as a dessert wine. Marsala wine is most often found in the Italian dessert Tiramisu. You can substitute veal for the chicken in this recipe.

1/2 cup flour
1 tablespoon *Creole Seasoning Blend* (page 146)
4 (4-ounce) chicken breast, boneless, skinless, and pounded thin
1 tablespoon olive oil
4 tablespoons butter, separated
3 cups sliced mushrooms
2 teaspoons garlic, minced
¾ cup marsala wine
1 cup *Chicken Stock* (page 146)
Salt and pepper to taste
Fresh parsley, chopped

In a shallow bowl, combine flour and Creole seasoning, mixing well. Quickly dredge the chicken in the flour, shaking to remove the excess. Heat olive oil in a large skillet over medium-high heat until very hot. Add 1 tablespoon butter and cook the chicken breast until golden brown on both sides, about 3 minutes each side. Remove chicken from the pan and keep warm. Add 1 tablespoon of the remaining butter to the pan and add mushrooms. Cook, stirring frequently, until mushrooms are golden brown around the edges and have given off their liquid. Add garlic and sauté for 1 minute. Add Marsala wine and bring to a boil, scraping the bottom of the pan with a wooden spoon to remove any bits from the bottom of the pan. When the wine is reduced by half, add the chicken stock or broth and cook for 3 minutes, or until the sauce has thickened slightly. Lower the heat to medium and return the chicken to the pan. Cook until the chicken is cooked through and the sauce has thickened, about 5-6 minutes. Add in the remaining 2 tablespoons butter and incorporate into the sauce. Salt and pepper to taste. Garnish the plate with parsley.

Chicken Oregano

This is another favorite Centola family dish. To borrow a phrase, this dish kicks up baked chicken a notch!! I do not know if my mother based this dish on Mosca's Chicken Grande or not. The good thing about this dish is that you can put it in the oven and do other things. Just check on it occasionally.

2 tablespoons fresh parsley, chopped
2 teaspoons fresh oregano, chopped
1 1/2 teaspoons salt
1/2 cup lemon juice

1 clove garlic, chopped
1/3 cup olive oil
Dash black pepper
1, 3- to 4-pound broiler-fryer, quartered

Preheat oven to 350°F. Mix all ingredients, brush on the chicken and bake in a 9x13-inch dish for 1½ hours.

Chicken Pontalba

Chef Paul Blange at Brennan's restaurant created this dish in the early 1950s. It is named for the Baroness Pontalba, who had built the two buildings that flank Jackson Square. The buildings house the oldest continually rented apartments in the United States. This dish is Creole cooking at its finest.

Olive oil
8 (6-ounce) chicken breasts, boneless and skinless
Creole Seasoning Blend (page 146)
1/2 cup butter
4 tablespoons garlic, minced
2 cups onion, chopped
2 cups green onion, chopped
1 1/2 cups ham, diced
2 cups mushrooms, sliced
1 1/2 cups potatoes, diced and deep-fried about 2 minutes
3 tablespoons fresh parsley, chopped
3/4 cup white wine
3 cups *Béarnaise Sauce* (page 107)

Preheat oven to 175°F. In a large skillet, pour enough olive oil to cover the bottom of the pan. Season the chicken with Creole seasoning. Sauté chicken over medium heat until done, about 4-5 minutes on each side. Remove the chicken and keep warm in oven. In a sauté pan, melt butter and sauté the garlic, onions, ham, and mushrooms until the mushrooms are brown. Add wine and reduce by 1/3. Add fried potatoes and parsley and cook 2 minutes. Put 1/8 of the potato mixture in the center of a plate. Place the chicken breast on top. Top with a generous amount of Béarnaise sauce.

Fried Chicken

What makes fried chicken a New Orleans dish? Al Copeland created Popeye's Fried Chicken in New Orleans. His spicy chicken changed the way the world ate fried chicken. This is my take of that chicken.

Canola oil
2 fryer chickens, cut into 8 pieces each
Creole Seasoning Blend (page 146)
1 cup buttermilk
4 eggs
1/3 cup water
1 cup flour
1 tablespoon granulated garlic
2 teaspoons granulated onion
2 teaspoons paprika
2 teaspoons cayenne pepper

Preheat large skillet filled with 2 inches of oil to 350°F. Wash chicken pieces and pat dry. Sprinkle generously with Creole seasoning. In a medium bowl, combine buttermilk, eggs and water: mix well. Mix dry seasonings with flour. Dip chicken pieces in buttermilk mixture and then dredge in flour, shaking off the excess. Fry chicken for approximately 10-15 minutes until brown on both sides. Chicken is done when juice that runs out after poking with a fork is clear. Drain well on paper towels before serving.

leg of lamb

Whenever I think of lamb, I think of my grandma, Ole. My mother's mother would occasionally cook leg of lamb. She would always invite me to eat with her, because she knew I loved to eat lamb. This recipe is as close to hers as I can remember. I consider myself lucky to have been surrounded by many wonderful cooks.

1 whole leg of lamb, about 6-9 pounds
20 cloves garlic, large ones cut in half lengthwise
Fresh rosemary
Fresh thyme
Creole Seasoning Blend (page 146)
Olive oil
Red wine

Prep

Prepare leg by removing most of the visible fat. Cut slits into the top portion of the roast with a small sharp knife. Insert garlic clove into each slit and push down with finger until it is no longer visible. Rub the herbs and Creole seasoning all over the surface. Do the same with olive oil. Splash with wine and rub again. Cover and let meat marinate for at least 3 hours or overnight in the refrigerator. Remove from refrigerator 1 hour before roasting.

Roasting

Preheat oven to 450°F. Place lamb in a shallow roasting pan. Roast for 10-15 minutes for initial searing, and then reduce temperature to 350°F. Continue roasting for 8 minutes per pound for rare, 10 minutes per pound for medium, or 18 minutes per pound for well done. Baste occasionally with pan juices. Remove roast from oven when done. Tent with aluminum foil and let rest 10-20 minutes before carving. Meanwhile, reduce the liquids in the pan and deglaze to get all the bits off the bottom of the pan. Add wine or water if necessary.

Osso Buco

Osso Buco is translated bone with a hole, referring to the marrow in the bone. This is the ultimate roasted veal dish. There are two versions. The older version is seasoned with cinnamon and bay leaf. The modern version is the one you will likely find. Here is that version.

½ cup flour
Creole Seasoning Blend (page 146)
4 pieces veal shank with bone, cut to 3 inches
3 tablespoons olive oil
3 tablespoons butter
1 medium onion, chopped
1/2 cup celery, chopped
1/2 cup carrots, chopped
4 cloves garlic, chopped
2 bay leaves
3 tablespoons fresh parsley, minced
1 cup marsala wine
2 cups *Chicken Stock* (page 146)
2 tomatoes, peeled, seeded and chopped

In a large shallow bowl, season flour with Creole seasoning. Dredge veal shanks in the flour, shaking off the excess. In a large skillet or Dutch oven, over medium heat, heat the oil and butter. Sear the shanks on all sides. Make sure the bones do not touch the pan to keep the marrow in the bones. Add more oil and butter, if needed. Remove the browned shanks and set aside. Add onions, celery, carrots, garlic, bay leaves and parsley to the pan and cook until soft. Season with Creole seasoning. Raise the heat to high. Add the wine and deglaze the pan. Return the shanks to the pan. Add the stock and tomato and drizzle with olive oil. Reduce heat to low, cover and cook for about 1 1/2 hours or until the meat is tender. Baste the meat a few times while cooking. Remove the cover and continue to simmer for 10 minutes to reduce the sauce.

Panéed Veal

This is a simple yet delicious dish. It is basically veal coated with breadcrumbs and pan-fried. You can panne any meat with great results. This dish became popular in New Orleans restaurants in the late 1970s. As easy as it is to prepare, I am sure the chefs were glad it became popular.

8 (3-ounce) slices of veal
1/2 cup flour
1 1/2 teaspoons *Creole Seasoning Blend* (page 146)
2 eggs, beaten
3/4 cup seasoned breadcrumbs
3/4 cup grated Parmesan cheese
Olive oil
Fresh parsley, chopped

Pound the veal with a meat tenderizer between 2 pieces of plastic wrap until each piece is doubled in size. Mix the flour and Creole seasoning together. In another platter, mix the breadcrumbs and Parmesan cheese together. Lightly dust the veal in the flour. Dip the veal in the egg, shaking off the excess. Dredge veal through the breadcrumb mixture, shaking off the excess. Heat about 1/2-inch olive oil in a heavy skillet over medium-high heat. It is hot enough when a pinch of breadcrumbs fries quickly. Cook the veal, not crowding the pan, for about 1 1/2 minutes per side, or until golden brown. Remove and drain on paper towels. Garnish with parsley when serving.

Pork Chops and Artichoke

This is another recipe from my mother Mona. This is another dish, which can be put in the oven and left alone. This is a classic Creole Italian dish that you will not find in a restaurant. It is great home cooking.

4 pork chops
Garlic salt, to taste
Black pepper, to taste
1 can artichoke hearts, chopped
Seasoned bread crumbs
Parmesan cheese, grated

Preheat oven to 325°F. Sprinkle pork chops with garlic salt and black pepper. Cover chops with artichoke hearts. Sprinkle the artichoke with breadcrumbs and Parmesan cheese. Cover with aluminum foil and bake for 1 hour. Uncover and bake 20 minutes more or until browned.

Turkey Poulet

This is the perfect after holiday meal. It is an excellent way to use leftover turkey, and it is easy to make. The only real cooking is the bacon and white sauce. I usually cannot wait for Thanksgiving or Christmas because I know this dish will be in my near future.

8 pieces bread, lightly toasted
24 slices bacon, cooked crisp
24 ounces turkey, cooked
Double recipe of *White Sauce* (page 111)
Fresh Parmesan cheese, grated

Preheat oven to 350°F. For each serving, place 2 pieces of toast side by side on an oven proof plate. Place 3 slices of bacon and 3 ounces of turkey on each piece of toast. Cover with white sauce. Sprinkle with Parmesan cheese and bake for 15 minutes.

Veal Andrew

This dish is named for my godchild, Andrew. At eleven years old, he is a very adventurous eater. So, I came up with this dish for him. I know he would eat anything with crawfish in it. Andrew, this one is for you.

8 (3-ounce) slices of veal
1/2 cup flour
1 1/2 teaspoons *Creole Seasoning Blend* (page 146)
3/4 cup seasoned breadcrumbs
3/4 cup grated Parmesan cheese
2 eggs, beaten
Olive oil
Fresh parsley, chopped
Cream of Crawfish Sauce (page 107)

Pound the veal with a meat tenderizer between 2 pieces of plastic wrap until each piece is doubled in size. Mix the flour and Creole seasoning together. In another platter, mix the breadcrumbs and Parmesan cheese together. Lightly dust the veal in the flour. Dip the veal in the egg, shaking off the excess. Dredge veal through the breadcrumb mixture, shaking off the excess. Heat about 1/2-inch olive oil in a heavy skillet over medium-high heat. It is hot enough when a pinch of breadcrumbs fries quickly. Cook the veal, not crowding the pan, for about 1 1/2 minutes per side, or until golden brown. Remove and drain on paper towels. Top with crawfish sauce and garnish with parsley.

Veal Marie

This is my version of my favorite entrée from LeRuth's restaurant. Veal Marie was named after Chef Warren Leruth's wife. This dish was originally served with king crab leg meat. I think the best crabmeat comes from the blue crab, which is native to the waters around New Orleans. My recipe includes jumbo lump blue crabmeat. Whichever crabmeat you use, you have a five-star dish.

Double *White Sauce* recipe substituting heavy cream for the milk (page 111)
1 pound jumbo lump crabmeat
8 (3-ounce) slices of veal
1/2 cup flour
1 1/2 teaspoons *Creole Seasoning Blend* (page 146)
Canola oil
8 *Crêpes* (page 146)
Fresh parsley, chopped

Make the white sauce, then add the crabmeat. Keep warm. Pound the veal with a meat tenderizer between 2 pieces of plastic wrap until each piece is doubled in size. Mix the flour and Creole seasoning together. Lightly dust the veal in the flour. Add enough oil to a large skillet to coat the bottom. Heat over medium heat. Sauté the veal for 1 1/2 minutes on each side or until golden brown. Do not overcrowd the pan. Cook the veal in multiple batches, adding oil to the pan as needed. Keep veal warm. To serve, place two pieces of veal on serving plate. Top with a crêpe; spoon crabmeat sauce over the crêpe. Garnish with parsley.

Veal Parmesan

This is one of the iconic Italian dishes. Ask anyone to name three Italian dishes and the probable answer will be spaghetti and meatballs, lasagna and veal Parmesan. This dish is also easily made with chicken breast. There is nothing like cutting into a piece of veal Parmesan and having strings of melted mozzarella cheese stretching from the plate to your fork.

1 stick butter, melted
3/4 cup seasoned breadcrumbs
3/4 cup Parmesan cheese, grated
4 4-ounce slices of veal, pounded thin
3 Eggs, beaten
Italian Red Sauce (page 109)
4 slices mozzarella cheese
Cooked pasta

Preheat oven to 400°F. Put melted butter in a 13x9-inch baking dish. Combine breadcrumbs with Parmesan cheese, and mix well. Dip veal in egg, then coat with breadcrumb/cheese mixture. Repeat the last step, double breading the veal. Put in baking dish and cook for 5-6 minutes on each side. Pour the sauce around the veal, and cook for 5 more minutes. Cover each piece of veal with a slice of mozzarella cheese. Cook until cheese is melted. Serve with pasta topped with sauce from pan.

Veal Piccata

Piccata in Italian means to be pounded flat. This is a quick and elegant dish. The key to the dish is making sure the stock or broth is hot before you add it to the pan. You can also do this with chicken; just make sure the chicken is pounded thin. If not, it will take longer to cook.

Flour
Creole Seasoning Blend (page 146)
4 (4-ounce veal) slices pounded thin
3 tablespoons butter divided
2 tablespoons fresh parsley, chopped
2 tablespoons hot *Chicken Stock* (page 146)
1 Tablespoon lemon juice

Heat oven to 175°F. Season flour with Creole seasoning. Heat large sauté pan over medium heat. Dredge the veal in flour, shaking off the excess. Melt 2 tablespoons of the butter in the pan. Turn the heat to medium-high and add the veal, cooking it quickly. When the meat is done, place on platter in the oven to keep hot. Add the parsley, lemon juice, remaining butter, and hot stock or broth to pan. Stir well and as soon as the sauce is bubbling, place veal on serving plates and pour sauce over top. Serve immediately.

Veal Saltimbocca

Saltimbocca literally means "jump in the mouth." As good as this dish is, it will seem like it is jumping into your mouth. This is another quick veal dish. You want to make sure you remove the toothpicks from the veal before you serve it.

4 (4-ounce) veal slices, pounded thin
4 slices of prosciutto or other thin ham
4 fresh sage leaves
4 toothpicks
4 tablespoons butter
1/2 cup fresh parsley, minced
Creole Seasoning Blend (page 146)
1/2 cup white wine
1 tablespoon capers (optional)

On each slice of veal, place a slice of prosciutto and sage leaf. Secure with a toothpick. Melt butter in a large skillet over medium heat. Add the veal slices; brown on both sides. When done, season veal with parsley and Creole seasoning. Remove from pan and keep warm. Add wine and capers to the pan. Increase heat to medium-high. Deglaze the pan. Put veal on serving plate, remove toothpick and cover with sauce. Serve immediately.

Pasta

Pasta arrived in Louisiana in the late 1800s, when a large number of immigrants from Sicily began to settle in New Orleans. This was a great marriage because the great seafood of the area was meant to top pasta. Crabmeat, shrimp, oysters, crawfish, chicken, and tasso all appear in the recipes that follow. Since I have Italian blood running through my body, this is probably my favorite section of the cookbook--of course, not counting the desserts.

Chicken Pesto Pasta
Crabmeat Alfredeaux
Crawfish Fettuccini
Lasagna
Linguini with Clam Sauce
Meatballs and Spaghetti
Oysters Bordelaise
Pasta Jambalaya
Shrimp and Tasso Pasta
Shrimp Fra Diavolo
Shrimp Pasta Lorraine
Shrimp Scampi

Chicken Pesto Pasta

This is a very rich and filling dish. You start with an Alfredo sauce, and then you add Pesto sauce to it. Traditional Pesto sauce is made with basil, garlic, Parmesan cheese, pine nuts, and Olive oil. This turns the sauce a pale green. The flavor is unbelievable.

Olive oil
3 6-ounce chicken breast, boneless skinless and cut into strips
4 cups *Alfredo Sauce* (page 107)
4 tablespoons *Pesto* (page 110)
4 tablespoons *Italian Red Sauce* or any *Pasta Sauce* (page 109)
12 ounces penne pasta, cooked al dente
4 ounces smoked Gouda cheese, grated
4 ounces provolone cheese, grated

Put enough olive oil to cover the bottom of a large skillet. Over medium heat, sauté the chicken breast. In a large pan, heat Alfredo sauce; add the pesto, mixing well. When chicken is done, add it to the sauce mixture. After draining the penne, return it to the pot it was boiled in. Over low heat, add the chicken and sauce mixture; mix well. Put 1 tablespoon of red sauce on the bottom of the serving bowl. Divide the chicken and pasta equally among the 4 bowls. Top the pasta with one ounce of Gouda and provolone cheeses.

Crabmeat Alfredeaux

Most chain restaurants rename the Alfredo sauce Alfredeaux to make you think that it is straight from the Bayou. Just changing the spelling of a sauce does not make it a Cajun dish; I have tasted many Alfredeaux sauces that have very little or no seasoning at all. Crabmeat is delicate meat. If you use too much seasoning, it will overpower the flavor of the crab. That is why I keep a collection of hot sauces. If someone wants more heat, they can add it.

1/2-pound butter
1 tablespoon garlic, minced
1 1/2 cup milk
1 1/2 cup heavy cream
2 1/4 cup Parmesan cheese, grated
1 tablespoon black pepper
1 tablespoon *Creole Seasoning Blend* (page 146)
1/2 teaspoon liquid crab boil (optional)
1 pound lump crabmeat, cleaned of shells
8 ounces spaghetti cooked al dente

In a large saucepan over medium heat, sauté garlic in butter for 3 minutes or golden brown. Add the milk and heavy cream. Heat until the edges start to bubble. Slowly add Parmesan cheese and mix until well blended. Add black pepper, Creole seasoning, and crab boil. Cook for 5 minutes or until desired thickness. Add crabmeat and turn off heat. After two minutes. Serve over cooked spaghetti.

Crawfish Fettuccini

I am still a little surprised when I run into someone who does not like crawfish. I quickly realize that most people have not tasted crawfish. One of the most common statements I hear that it is "too much work for such little meat." You do not have to have a crawfish boil to have crawfish tails. In most grocery stores, you can buy a package of frozen crawfish tails. They will work great in the following recipe.

1 pound fettuccini, cooked al dente
Olive oil
2 tablespoons butter
1 pound crawfish tails
Seafood Seasoning Blend (page 148)
2 tablespoons red onion, minced
1 tablespoon garlic, minced
1 tablespoon Crystal hot sauce
2 cups heavy cream
Parmesan cheese, grated
1/4 cup green onion, chopped
Fresh parsley, chopped

Cook pasta and drain. Put back in pan and sprinkle with olive oil. In a large sauté pan over medium heat, melt the butter. Sauté the crawfish in the butter for 2 minutes. Season with seafood seasoning. Add the red onions and garlic and continue sautéing for 1 minute. Stir in the hot sauce and cream. Bring the liquid up to a boil and reduce to a simmer. Simmer for about 8 minutes or until the sauce thickens. Pour the crawfish mixture over the pasta and toss. Season with seafood seasoning. Fold in the Parmesan cheese and green onion. Garnish with parsley.

Lasagna

This is Italian comfort food at its finest. There are many variations of lasagna. This one is simple but delicious. A great variation to try is to substitute seafood for the meat and Alfredo sauce for the red sauce. I am saving that recipe for another time.

1 pound ground chuck
1/2-pound ground Italian sausage

1 medium onion, diced
5 cloves garlic, minced
Italian Red Sauce (page 109)
1 box lasagna noodles, cooked al dente
1 pound mozzarella cheese, shredded
Parmesan cheese, grated

Preheat oven to 375°F. Brown ground meat, sausage, onion, and garlic. Drain fat. Add red sauce and cook for 5 minutes.

Assembly

Put a thin layer of sauce on the bottom of a 13x9-inch baking dish. Layer in the following order: pasta, meat sauce, mozzarella cheese, and Parmesan cheese. Make sure that your last layer are mozzarella and Parmesan cheeses. Bake for 20–25 minutes or until the cheese on top is melted.

Linguini with White Clam Sauce

Fresh clams are not found locally in the waters that surround New Orleans, but are found along the Atlantic shores of the New England states. This dish, however, is still a favorite of mine. It is one that can be prepared quickly. This is one of the dishes that I prepared a lot when I was in my teens. I hope you enjoy it as much as I do.

3 tablespoons butter
1 tablespoon garlic, chopped
3 tablespoons flour
3 (6 ½ ounce) cans chopped clams, save juice
1 (8-ounce) bottle clam juice
1 teaspoon fresh parsley, chopped
1 teaspoon fresh basil, chopped
1/4 teaspoon fresh oregano, chopped
8 ounces linguini, cooked al dente
Fresh Parmesan cheese, grated

Cook pasta, drain, and return it to pot in which it was cooked. In a medium saucepan over medium heat, sauté garlic in butter until golden brown. Mix in the flour and cook for a few minutes to cook out the flour taste. Add the clam juice, reserved from cans and bottle, and seasonings. Cover and bring to a boil. Lower heat to medium-low and simmer for 5 minutes. Add clams and heat for 2 minutes. Pour sauce over pasta; toss until the pasta is coated. Top individual portions with Parmesan cheese.

Meatballs and Spaghetti

Nothing says Italian like meatballs and spaghetti. This dish is so iconic that Walt Disney had *Lady and the Tramp* sharing a plate of meatballs and spaghetti on their date in the alley of an Italian restaurant. There is nothing like eating meatballs fresh out of the oven. Words cannot describe the flavor. Have one before you put it in the red sauce. You will be glad you did.

1 pound ground chuck
1/2 pound ground Italian sausage
1/2 pound ground veal
1 medium onion, minced
6 cloves garlic, minced
2 tablespoons fresh basil, chopped
2 tablespoons fresh oregano, chopped
1 tablespoon salt
1 tablespoon black pepper
2 eggs
3/4 cup breadcrumbs
Italian Red Sauce (page 109)
1 pound spaghetti, cooked al dente

Preheat oven to 375°F. Mix meat together in a large mixing bowl. Add onion, garlic, basil, oregano, salt, and pepper; mix well. Add breadcrumbs and eggs; mix well. Roll meat into 2-inch balls. Bake in oven for 20 minutes. Add meatballs to warm red sauce and cook for 10 minutes. Serve over hot spaghetti.

Oysters Bordelaise

Oysters are a perfect addition to pasta. I cannot think of a better sauce for oysters than a New Orleans style bordelaise. You can prepare this dish in the time it takes to cook pasta. Oysters should not be overcooked. They become chewy when they are cooked too long. So, remember, cook the oysters until they start curling around the edges.

1/4 cup olive oil
2 dozen large fresh oysters
3 tablespoons butter, softened
1/4 cup green onion, chopped
2 tablespoon garlic, minced
Pinch *Creole Seasoning Blend* (page 146)
1 pound spaghetti, cooked al dente
3 tablespoons fresh parsley, minced

In a large skillet over medium heat, heat the olive oil until it shimmers. Add the oysters, cooking them by shaking the pan and making them roll around until they plump up. Add green onion and garlic; cook until the green onions are wilted (about 2 minutes). Add the cooked, drained spaghetti to the pan and toss with a large fork to distribute pan contents among the pasta. Serve with parsley.

Pasta Jambalaya

This dish was created in the kitchen of Mr. B's Bistro in the French Quarter of New Orleans. The idea was to replace the rice in Jambalaya with pasta. This dish was quickly copied around New Orleans. Here is my version of it.

1/4 cup olive oil
1 1/2 teaspoons chili powder
1 tablespoon cumin
6 ounces andouille sausage, cut into bite-sized discs
6 ounces chicken breast, cut into bite sized pieces
1 tablespoon garlic, chopped
1/8 cup red onion, cut julienne
1/8 cup yellow bell pepper, cut julienne
1 1/2 cups marinara sauce, warmed
1 pound tricolor fusilli (spiral) pasta, cooked al dente
Shredded provolone cheese
Shredded smoked Gouda cheese

Combine olive oil, chili powder and cumin. Sauté andouille and chicken in oil mixture until the chicken has lost its raw color. Add onion, bell pepper and garlic; cook until garlic is golden. Add marinara sauce; bring to a boil. Place warm pasta into a large bowl and cover with the sauce. Mix well and divide into 4 bowls. Top with cheeses.

Shrimp and Tasso Pasta

This is my version of the Shrimp and Tasso Pasta that is served at Copeland's of New Orleans. The gentleman who developed Popeye's Fried Chicken, the late Al Copeland, started this chain. Al put together a team of New Orleans chefs to develop his menu, one of them being Chef Warren Leruth. Al was a great man and is missed by all.

1 tablespoon garlic, minced
10 tablespoons butter, divided
2 cup heavy cream
½ cup Parmesan cheese, grated
2 dozen medium shrimp, peeled and deveined

¼ pound tasso, diced
8 ounces bow tie pasta, cooked al dente

In a large saucepan over medium heat, sauté garlic in 8 tablespoons butter for 3 minutes or golden brown. Add the heavy cream. Heat until the edges start to bubble. Slowly add Parmesan cheese and mix until well blended. In a medium sauté pan, sauté shrimp and tasso in remaining butter until shrimp are done. Add shrimp and tasso to sauce. Keep warm for 3 minutes. Serve over bow tie pasta.

Shrimp Fra Diavolo

"Fra Diavolo" is Italian for brother devil. This is a dish that you are not likely to find in Italy as it is an Italian-American creation. You can control the heat of this dish by adjusting the amount of red pepper flakes you use.

1 pound large shrimp, peeled and deveined
1 teaspoon *Seafood Seasoning Blen*d (page 148)
1 teaspoon crushed red pepper flakes
3 tablespoons olive oil
1 medium onion minced
1 (14 1/2 ounce) can diced tomatoes in tomato puree
1 cup dry white wine
3 cloves garlic, minced
1/4 teaspoon fresh oregano leaves, chopped
3 tablespoons fresh parsley, chopped
3 tablespoons fresh basil, chopped
8 ounces linguini, cooked al dente

In a large bowl, toss shrimp with seafood seasoning and red pepper flakes. In a large heavy skillet, heat the olive oil over medium heat. Add the shrimp and sauté until just cooked through, about two minutes. Using a slotted spoon, transfer the shrimp to a large plate and set aside. Add the onion to the same skillet and sauté until translucent, about 5 minutes. Add the tomatoes with their juices, wine, garlic, and oregano, and simmer until the sauce thickens slightly, about 10 minutes. Return the shrimp and any accumulated juices to the tomato mixture and toss to coat. Remove from heat and stir in the parsley and basil. Serve over linguini.

Shrimp Pasta Lorraine

Lorraine is my mother-in-law. She likes this dish so much; it seems like the only thing she wants me to cook for her. To honor her, I named the dish after her. This is a very special dish for me. It is the dish that I cooked for the meeting of my mother and mother-in-law.

2 pounds medium shrimp, peeled and deveined

2 tablespoons *Seafood Seasoning Blend* (page 148)
1/2 pound and 3 tablespoons butter, divided
1 tablespoon garlic, minced
2 cups milk
2 cups heavy cream
2 1/4 cup Parmesan cheese, grated
3 tablespoons fresh basil, chopped
3 tablespoons fresh oregano, chopped
2 tablespoons fresh parsley, chopped
8 ounces of cooked spaghetti, cooked al dente

Sprinkle shrimp with seafood seasoning and sauté in 3 tablespoons of butter until the shrimp start to turn pink. In a large saucepan over medium heat, sauté garlic in 1/2-pound butter for 3 minutes or golden brown. Add the milk and heavy cream. Heat until the edges start to bubble. Slowly add Parmesan cheese and mix until well blended. Add shrimp, basil, oregano, and parsley to sauce. Cook for 10 minutes. Serve over spaghetti.

Shrimp Scampi

Shrimp Scampi translated is "shrimp shrimp." Traditionally, scampi is cooked in garlic and butter. It is an excellent dish served over pasta. I always serve this with French bread so every drop of sauce can be mopped up and eaten.

1 1/2 pounds medium shrimp, peeled and deveined
Seafood Seasoning Blend (page 148)
1/3 cup butter
4 tablespoons garlic, minced
1/4 cup green onions, sliced
1/4 cup dry white wine
2 tablespoons lemon juice
2 tablespoons fresh parsley, chopped
8 ounces cooked pasta, cooked al dente

Coat shrimp with seafood seasoning. Heat butter in a large skillet over medium heat. Cook garlic 1 or 2 minutes or until softened but not browned. Add shrimp, green onion, wine, and lemon juice: cook until shrimp are pink and firm, about 1 to 2 minutes on each side. Do not overcook. Add parsley and serve over pasta.

Sauces

A sauce on a dish can transform the dish from a good one to a great one. In some restaurants, there is a person whose sole job is to make sauces and is known as a saucier. There are 5 (some say 6) mother sauces from which there are hundreds of variations. They are the white sauce or béchamel, velouté, espagnole, hollandaise, and mayonnaise. The 6th one that came later is the tomato sauce. Many of the sauces that follow are unique to New Orleans.

Alfredo Sauce
Béarnaise Sauce
Cream of Crawfish Sauce
Hickory Sauce
Hollandaise Sauce
Italian Red Sauce
Lemon Sauce
Meunière Sauce
New Orleans Bordelaise
Pesto
Roasted Garlic Crawfish Sauce
White Chocolate Sauce
White Sauce (Béchamel)

Alfredo Sauce

1 tablespoon fresh garlic, chopped
1/2 pound butter
1 1/2 cups milk
1 1/2 cups heavy cream
4 1/2 cups Parmesan cheese, grated
1 tablespoon black pepper

In a large saucepan, sauté garlic in butter for 2 minutes. Add the milk and heavy cream. Heat until the edges start to bubble. Slowly add the Parmesan cheese and mix until well blended. Add the black pepper and cook for 5 minutes.

Béarnaise Sauce

This sauce is great with meat and fish.

2 tablespoons dried tarragon
3/4 cup red wine vinegar
2 tablespoons shallots, minced
2 sticks margarine
1 stick butter
2 egg yolks
1 whole egg
1 1/2 teaspoons lemon juice
1/2 teaspoon apple cider vinegar
1/2 teaspoon ground white pepper
1/4 teaspoon cayenne pepper

In a heavy skillet over medium heat, sauté tarragon, red wine vinegar and shallots for 10-15 minutes, or until the mixture becomes paste-like and remove from heat. Melt margarine and butter over medium heat. Bring to a boil, remove from heat and allow to cool. In a blender, blend egg yolks, egg, vinegar, cayenne, white pepper, and lemon juice. With blender on, pour melted margarine mixture slowly into other ingredients. Blend to thicken. Add the tarragon mixture and blend well.

Cream of Crawfish Sauce

1/2 cup crawfish tails, slightly chopped
2 tablespoons *Creole Seasoning Blend* (page 146)
2/3 cup onions, minced

1 teaspoon Worcestershire sauce
2 cups heavy cream
2 tablespoons butter, cut in to pieces

Coat crawfish with Creole seasoning. Combine crawfish, onion and Worcestershire sauce in a sauté pan. Sauté for 2 minutes. Add heavy cream and reduce for 10 minutes. Add butter; stir until butter is melted and incorporated.

Hickory Sauce

Great on burgers, this sauce has the flavor you will return to time after time.

1 quart BBQ sauce
1 quart chili sauce
1/2 cup honey
2 tablespoons onion, minced
1/4 cup liquid smoke
1 teaspoon salt
1 teaspoon white pepper
1/2 teaspoon yellow mustard

Combine all ingredients and mix thoroughly. Keep refrigerated between uses.

Hollandaise Sauce

2 sticks margarine
1 stick butter
2 egg yolks
1 whole egg
1 1/2 teaspoons lemon juice
1/2 teaspoon apple cider vinegar
1/2 teaspoon ground white pepper
1/4 teaspoon cayenne pepper

Melt butter and margarine over medium heat. Bring to a boil, remove from heat and allow to cool. Blend egg yolks, egg, vinegar, cayenne, white pepper, and lemon juice. With blender on, pour melted margarine mixture slowly into other ingredients. Blend to thick.

Italian Red Sauce

1 tablespoon butter
1 tablespoon fresh garlic, minced
1/4 cup onion, minced
1 can (29 ounce) tomato sauce
1 can (6 ounce) tomato paste
1 tablespoon Italian seasonings
1 tablespoon fresh oregano, chopped
2 teaspoons fresh basil, chopped
1 teaspoon fresh parsley, chopped
2 tablespoons sugar

In a medium saucepan over medium heat, melt butter. Sauté garlic and onions in butter until onion are soft. Add the tomato sauce and paste; mixing well, making sure the paste does not remain in lumps. Add the rest of the ingredients and mix well. Adjust the seasonings to taste. Cook for 5 minutes and serve.

Lemon Sauce

Every cook needs a great lemon sauce in one's repertoire. This lemon sauce definitely fits the bill.

1/4 cup lemon juice
1/4 cup Chablis wine
1/4 teaspoon Worcestershire sauce
3 cups heavy cream
1/2 teaspoons salt
1/8 teaspoon white pepper

In a medium sauté pan over medium heat, combine the lemon juice and Chablis, reducing by half. In a large saucepan, combine the rest of ingredients. Over medium heat, reduce by half. Whip the wine mixture and reduce by half. Keep warm until it is used.

Meunière Sauce

2 sticks butter
2 tablespoons lemon juice
2 teaspoons Worcestershire sauce

In a small saucepan over low heat, melt butter until it stops bubbling and the milk solids at the bottom of the pan begin to brown. Carefully add the lemon juice and Worcestershire sauce; the butter will foam. Cook until the foam subsides.

New Orleans Bordelaise Sauce

Traditionally, Bordelaise sauce is made with red wine. In New Orleans, we do it a little differently. There is no wine in the New Orleans style sauce.

1/4 cup butter
2 tablespoons olive oil
4 cloves garlic, minced
1/2 teaspoon salt
1/4 teaspoon black pepper
1 tablespoon fresh parsley, chopped

In a small saucepan over low heat, melt the butter. Add the olive oil; warm for 3 minutes. Add the garlic, salt and pepper. Cook over low heat for 5 minutes or until the garlic begins to brown. Turn off the heat and quickly remove the garlic with a strainer. Add the parsley and serve.

Pesto

This sauce is great over warm pasta. When mixed with cream, it tastes great over fish.

1 1/2 cups fresh basil
3 tablespoons fresh garlic, chopped
1/4 cup pine nuts
1/4 cup Parmesan cheese, grated
1/4 cup lemon juice
1/2 cup olive oil

Place all items in a blender and blend into a paste.

Roasted Garlic Crawfish Sauce

3/4 cup crawfish tails, slightly chopped
2 tablespoons *Creole Seasoning Blend* (page 146)
1/2 cup onion, minced
1 tablespoon Worcestershire sauce
2 cups heavy cream

3 tablespoons roasted garlic
2 tablespoons butter, cut in to pieces

Coat crawfish with Creole seasoning. Combine crawfish, onion and Worcestershire sauce in a sauté pan. Sauté for 2 minutes. Add heavy cream and roasted garlic. Reduce for 10 minutes. Remove from fire. Add butter and stir until butter is melted and incorporated.

White Chocolate Sauce

This dessert sauce is a great addition to most desserts.

8 ounces white chocolate chips
1/3 cup heavy cream

In a double boiler, over barely simmering water, melt chocolate until smooth. Remove from heat and mix in the heavy cream. Keep warm. To store, let cool slightly and store in an airtight container in the refrigerator. To reheat, in a double boiler, melt over barely simmering water and stir until smooth.

White Sauce (Béchamel)

This is the most versatile of the mother sauces. By adding shredded cheese, you have what is known as a Mornay sauce. Because of the lack of bold flavors, anything added to this sauce brings a new flavor to the sauce.

2 tablespoon butter
2 tablespoons flour
1/4 teaspoon salt
Dash white pepper
Dash nutmeg
1 1/2 cups milk

In a small saucepan over low heat, melt butter. Stir in the flour, salt, pepper, and nutmeg. Cook until evenly combined. After the mixture is combined with no lumps, slowly add the milk, stirring constantly with a wire whisk until evenly blended. Stir sauce over medium heat until the mixture bubbles across the entire surface. Cook and stir for a couple more minutes to completely cook the flour into the sauce.

Side Dishes

Side dishes keep the excitement going in the kitchen. This is where you can use almost anything to make a side dish. It can be as simple as Cajun Boiled Potatoes or as complex as Twice Baked Potatoes. Rice, vegetables, pasta, and even apples, can be used in preparing side dishes. The right-side dish can make a good meal a perfect meal.

Brabant Potatoes
Cajun Boiled Potatoes
Carrots with Orange Sauce
Cinnamon Pecan Apples
Dirty Rice
Fried Okra
Fried Onion Rings
Fried Parsley
Garlic Mashed Potatoes
Hash Brown Potato Casserole
Herb Rice Pilaf
Hurgy Lurgy
Hushpuppies
Maque Choux
Oyster Dressing
Sautéed Mushrooms and Onions
Sweet Potato Casserole
Vegetable Surprise

Brabant Potatoes

Brabant Potatoes look like fried potatoes. These fried potatoes have been tossed in a garlic butter that adds loads of flavor. This dish can be found in some of the best restaurants in New Orleans. So, if you are looking for a new way to serve fried potatoes, this is the way to go.

3 pounds potatoes
4 cloves garlic, chopped
1 stick butter
2 teaspoons fresh parsley, chopped
Salt and pepper to taste

Preheat deep fryer to 375°F. Peel and wash potatoes. Cut potatoes into small cubes (1x1-inch), rinse in cool water and drain. Fry potatoes until golden brown. Drain on paper towel and set aside in a medium mixing bowl. In a medium sauté pan over medium heat, sauté garlic in butter until golden brown. Pour butter and garlic over potatoes. Add parsley and mix well. Season with salt and pepper and serve.

Cajun Boiled Potatoes

I love potatoes that have been boiled with seafood. They develop a flavor that makes me eat more than I should. The only problem was that you had to have a seafood boil to have them. I developed this recipe for those times between boils. This is as close as you can get without the seafood.

1/2-gallon water
12 small red potatoes
2 tablespoons salt
2 ounces Zatarain's liquid crab boil
10 cloves garlic, peeled
1/2 teaspoon cayenne pepper

In a 6-quart pot, add all ingredients over high heat. Bring to a boil then lower heat to medium-low. Cook for about 15 minutes or until the potatoes are soft.

Carrots with Orange Glaze

My mom was always trying to get us kids to eat our vegetables. This is one of the recipes that she used. This is also one of the dishes she would prepare for covered dish (potluck) dinners. I am sure you can get almost anyone to eat carrots with this recipe.
2 cans small baby carrots or sliced carrots, drained
1/2 cup orange juice

1/2 cup sugar
1 tablespoon cornstarch
1 teaspoon salt
1 tablespoon orange zest
2 tablespoons butter

Preheat oven to 350°F. Place carrots in a 2-quart casserole. In a medium bowl, combine orange juice, sugar, cornstarch, salt, and orange zest. Pour mixture over carrots. Add butter and bake, covered, for 30 minutes.

Cinnamon Pecan Apples

This is a side dish that works great with BBQ ribs. It also tastes great on top of ice cream as a dessert. This is how this dish was used at Cannon's restaurant. It makes a great filling for a pecan apple pie.

4 1/2 pounds escalloped apples, thawed
1 tablespoon cinnamon ground
8 tablespoons butter
1/2 cup pecan pieces
1/8 teaspoon nutmeg, ground

Melt butter, and then add cinnamon and nutmeg. Add pecans and stir. Evenly distribute butter mixture on top of apples and mix softly. Warm apples before serving.

Dirty Rice

Dirty rice, or rice dressing, is a tradition on most holiday tables. In my family, we always had dirty rice on the holiday table. I was very fortunate a few years ago when my brother Ken found something that he thought I would like to have. It was the pan in which my mom had made her dirty rice. It brings back good memories every time I use that pan.

1 pound ground chuck
1/2 cup green onions, chopped
6 cups cooked rice
3 tablespoons *Creole Seasoning Blend* (page 146)
2 cups *Chicken Stock* (page 146)

Brown ground meat over medium heat. Drain fat. Add the green onions and cook until soft. Add rice and mix well. Add Creole seasoning and mix well. Add stock and cook until it is all absorbed.

Fried Okra

Fried okra is a staple in the south. It is an excellent side dish for fried seafood. It is also very popular on buffets. It's not just for gumbo.

1 pound fresh okra
2 eggs, beaten
1/4 cup buttermilk
1 cup flour
1 cup cornmeal
2 teaspoons baking powder
1 1/2 teaspoons *Creole Seasoning Blend* (page 146)

Preheat deep fryer to 375°F. Wash and slice okra into bite sized pieces; pat dry with a paper towel. Combine eggs and buttermilk; add okra and let soak for 10 minutes. Combine flour, cornmeal, baking powder, and Creole seasoning. Drain okra, small portion at a time, using a slotted spoon. Dredge okra, small batches at a time, in the flour mixture. Cook until golden brown. Drain on paper towels and serve immediately.

Fried Onion Rings

My wife loves onion rings. No matter where we go, if there are fried onion rings on the menu, it will end up on our table. Some of the best onion rings I have had were at Popeye's. I don't know why they stopped making them. So, here is my copy of Popeye's onion rings.

3 pounds Spanish or Vidalia onions
2 cups flour, divided
3/4 teaspoon salt
1/8 teaspoon black pepper
1/8 teaspoon cayenne pepper
1/2 teaspoon baking powder
1 egg, beaten well
1/2 cup buttermilk
2 tablespoons *Creole Seasoning Blend* (page 146)

Preheat deep fryer to 365°F. Wash and peel onions; cut into 1/4-inch-thick rounds. Separate rounds into rings. In a bowl, combine 1/2 cup of the flour, seasonings and baking powder. In a measuring cup, whisk together egg and milk. Add the egg mixture to the flour mixture, blending well. In another bowl, mix remaining flour with Creole seasoning. Dip onions in the flour, then the batter, and then the flour again, shaking off the excess each time. Fry onion rings until golden brown, turning to brown on both sides. Drain on paper towels and serve.

Fried Parsley

The first time I saw this sitting on the platter with a rack of lamb at LeRuth's restaurant, I could not believe my eyes! I could not believe that this five-star restaurant was serving this deep-fried parsley. When I tasted the fried parsley? I could not believe the taste. The parsley melted in my mouth. It left my mouth somewhat refreshed. The reason some restaurants put a sprig of parsley on the plate is to refresh your mouth for the next course.

1 bunch fresh curly parsley
Creole Seasoning Blend (page 146)

Preheat a deep fryer to 350°F. Clip the parsley leaving, at most, a 1/2-inch piece of stem. Make sure that the parsley is dry. Place a handful of parsley in the oil. Be careful, because the oil will pop. Remove the parsley after 15 seconds. Drain on a paper towel. Season with the Creole seasoning and serve.

Garlic Mashed Potatoes

The key to mashed potatoes is their fluffiness. Great mashed potatoes do not have lumps in them. To get the fluffiest mashed potatoes, you need to run the potatoes through either a potato ricer or a food mill. The ricer is great for a recipe serving 4. If you are cooking for a larger group, your best bet is a food mill.

3 pounds of potatoes, peeled and cut into small slices
48 ounces of chicken broth
1/4 cup granulated garlic
1 stick butter
1/2 cup heavy cream
Salt

Put the potato slices in a large pot. Cover potatoes with chicken broth. Add the granulated garlic. On high heat, bring the potatoes to a boil. Lower heat to medium low and cover the potatoes, cooking them until they are tender. Heat the heavy cream to take the chill off. Drain the potatoes. Mash the potatoes in a large bowl. Add the butter to potatoes and allow to melt. Add the heavy cream and mix until well blended. Salt to taste.

Hash Brown Potato Casserole

Here is another one of my mother's recipes. This dish works great for brunch or dinner. You can change it up by trying different cheeses. Also, you could use cream of mushroom soup in place of the cream of chicken.

2 pounds frozen hash brown potatoes
3/4 cup margarine, melted and separated
2 teaspoons black pepper
Salt to taste
1/2 cup onion, chopped
1 can (small) cream of chicken soup
1/4 cup milk
10 ounces American cheese, grated
2 cups corn flakes, crushed

Preheat oven to 350°F. Partially defrost potatoes. In a large sauté pan over medium heat, toss the potatoes with 1/2 cup melted margarine, salt and pepper. Add remaining ingredients. Transfer to a casserole dish. Mix corn flakes with the remaining melted margarine and spread on top of casserole. Bake for 45 minutes.

Herbed Rice Pilaf

This dish is one of the newer ones that I remember from childhood. Rice had always been served with gravy. This was the first time I saw rice uncovered. It has a great flavor with the different spices. This is a delicious way to serve rice.

1 cup long grain rice, uncooked
1 cup celery, chopped
3/4 cup onions, chopped
4 tablespoons butter
2 1/2 cups *Chicken Stock* (page 146)
1 (2-ounce) package Chicken Noodle Soup Mix
2 tablespoons fresh parsley, chopped
1/2 teaspoon fresh thyme, chopped
1/4 teaspoon rubbed sage
1/4 cup black pepper

In a large skillet over medium heat, cook the rice, celery and onion in butter, stirring constantly, until rice is browned. Stir in the next 6 ingredients, raise heat to high, and bring to a boil. Reduce heat to low, cover, and simmer for 15 minutes. Remove from heat and let stand, covered for 10 minutes.

Hurgy Lurgy

While working on my cookbook, I was looking for a recipe to honor my father. Unfortunately, he passed away when I was eleven. I turned to my older siblings to get their memories. This is one dish that got the most discussion. My father would cook on weekends. We had pancakes for breakfast and hamburgers for dinner on Saturdays. On Sundays, it was leftovers, or he would BBQ. This easy dish was a BBQ staple. Try it at your next BBQ. Here's to you, Dad.

8 ounces elbow macaroni, cooked
2 tablespoons fresh garlic, through a garlic press
1/3 cup olive oil
Fresh shredded Parmesan cheese (Optional)
Fresh parsley chopped (Optional)

Heat garlic in olive oil for 3 minutes. Toss pasta with oil & garlic. Serve while hot. Sprinkle with cheese and parsley.

Hushpuppies

No one knows how hushpuppies were first created. The most common story is that cooks would fry up bits of cornmeal to toss to the dogs on their way to the dining room in the main house. This was a time when the kitchens were not attached to the house. We may never know the real reason they were created, but we are glad they were invented. A seafood platter without hushpuppies is like red beans without rice.

1 cup yellow cornmeal
1 tablespoon flour
1/2 teaspoon baking soda
1 tablespoon baking powder
1 teaspoon salt
2 tablespoons onions, minced
1 egg, beaten
1 cup buttermilk

Preheat Deep Fryer to 350°F. Mix together all the dry ingredients. Add the onions, and then the milk and egg, mixing well. Immediately drop by the teaspoonful into the fryer. Fry until golden brown. Drain on paper towel before serving.
Note: You can make the batter in advance but you will have to add more cornmeal to the mix due to the moisture in the onions.

Maque Choux

Maque choux is a Cajun side dish with corn as the star. Corn was readily available to the Cajuns. It is a dish that varies depending on who is making it. The other key ingredient is the bacon drippings. This is what gives the flavor to the dish.

2 slices bacon, chopped
1 large onion, chopped
1 medium green bell pepper, chopped
2 1/2 cups tomatoes, peeled and chopped with juice
1 bay leaf
2 cups corn kernels, canned or fresh
1/2 teaspoon *Creole Seasoning Blend* (page 146)

In a large skillet over medium heat, cook bacon until crisp. Remove the bacon and set aside, reserving the drippings. Sauté the onions and bell peppers in drippings until tender. Add tomatoes and bay leaf; bring to a boil. Reduce heat and simmer about 5 minutes, stirring occasionally. Stir in corn; return to a boil. Reduce heat and simmer again for about 5 minutes. Add the Creole seasoning and bacon. Remove the bay leaf and serve.

Oyster Dressing

This is the perfect holiday side dish. Oysters are at their best around Thanksgiving and Christmas. Some people even use this stuffing inside their turkey. It is also great on the side of chicken and duck. Add it to your holiday menu.

2 teaspoons butter, to coat dish
1 pint oysters, reserving the liquor they come in
2 tablespoons canola oil
2 cups onion, chopped
1 cup green bell pepper, chopped
1 cup celery, chopped
2 teaspoons *Creole Seasoning Blend* (page 146)
2 bay leaves
1 tablespoon garlic, minced
1/4 cup fresh parsley, minced
1 cup *Chicken Stock* (page 146)
1/4 cup green onions, chopped
4 cups French bread, cut into 1-inch cubes
1/3 cup fresh Parmesan cheese, grated

Preheat oven to 375°F. Butter a 9x13-inch baking dish. Drain the oysters, reserving the oyster liquor. In a large skillet over medium-high heat, heat the oil. Add the onion, bell pepper, celery, and Creole seasoning; sauté for 5 minutes or until soft. Add the bay leaf, garlic and parsley, and sauté for 1 minute. Add the stock or broth and cook for 2-3 minutes, stirring constantly. Add the green onion, oyster liquor and the bread cubes. Stir to mix well; remove from heat. In a large mixing bowl, combine the bread mixture with the oysters and cheese. Stir to mix thoroughly. Pour the mixture into the baking dish and bake for 1 hour or until bubbly and golden brown. Remove the bay leaf before serving.

Sautéed Mushrooms and Onions

This is a dish that goes great with steak. My wife insists I make this dish every time I grill steaks. What is not to like about mushrooms and caramelized onions with a nice piece of ribeye. This is a simple addition to any menu.

6 tablespoons butter
8 ounces mushrooms, sliced
1 medium onion, cut in half and sliced thin
2 teaspoons *Creole Seasoning Blend* (page 146)

In a medium skillet over medium heat, melt the butter. Add the mushrooms, onions and Creole seasoning. Cook until the onions are caramelized, about 15 minutes, stirring frequently.

Sweet Potato Casserole

Louisiana is the third largest grower of sweet potatoes. Sweet potatoes are really starting to show its usability. Sweet potato french fries have been around for years. Now, they are starting to get recognized for their health benefits. It is a beneficial food for diabetics, of which I am one, for their help in stabilizing blood sugar and in lowering insulin resistance.

4 1/2 cups sweet potatoes, cooked and mashed
1 stick butter melted
1/3 cup milk
1 cup sugar
1/2 teaspoon vanilla extract
2 eggs, beaten
1 cup light brown sugar
1/2 cup flour
3 tablespoons butter
1 cup pecans, chopped

Preheat oven to 350 degrees. Grease a 9x13-inch baking pan. In a large bowl, mix together the sweet potatoes, 1 stick melted butter, milk, sugar, vanilla, and eggs. Spread sweet potatoes mixture into the baking dish. In a small bowl, mix together the brown sugar and flour. Cut and mix in 3 tablespoons butter until the mixture is creamy, then stir in the pecans. Sprinkle pecan mixture over sweet potatoes. Bake for 25 minutes or until golden brown.

Vegetable Surprise

The first time my mother and mother-in-law met was a dinner at my wife's home. While preparing the menu, I wanted to add a light vegetable to go with the shrimp pasta. I had seen someone prepare this dish while I was at work that day. It was quick and light--just what I was looking for. The Moms were pleased with my choice.

2 yellow squashes, quartered
1 zucchini, quartered
3 tablespoons butter
1/3 cup white wine
Salt, pepper and *Creole Seasoning Blend* to taste (page 146)

Over medium heat, melt butter in a large sauté pan. Allow butter to get hot, but not burnt. Add the squash and zucchini. Season with salt, pepper and Creole seasoning. Add wine and cover. Cook until vegetables are tender and all of the liquid has cooked off.

Desserts

I have yet to meet anyone who does not like the dessert course. New Orleans is known for having some famous desserts. Bananas Foster was created at Brennan's restaurant in the French Quarter. Aunt Sally's started making pralines in the 1930s. I may be partial but I think that some of the best desserts came from my own mother's kitchen. Her fudge pie recipe was always requested by whoever ate it. Her cheesecake was always the feature dessert during the holidays. Break out your sweet tooth and sample these wonderful desserts!

Cheesecake
Chocolate Pecan Pie
Crème Brûlée
Crêpes Alyson
Fudge Brownie Pie
Fudge Pie
Lemon Ice Box Pie
Peanut Butter Ice Box Pie
Pecan Pie
Sour Cream Cake
Sweet Potato Pie
Turtles
White Chocolate Bread Pudding
White Chocolate Mousse

Cheesecake

I have never eaten a better cheesecake than my mom's. Okay, so, I am biased. This dessert would always show up during the holidays. As I got older, I always wanted her cheesecake for my birthday. I have made this recipe many times, always to rave reviews and requests for the recipe.

Preheat oven to 375°F.

Crust
2 cups graham cracker crumbs
1 stick margarine, melted
½ cup sugar

Mix graham cracker crumbs, margarine and sugar together. Press into a 9-inch pie pan.

Filling
16 ounces cream cheese
2 eggs
2/3 cup sugar
1 teaspoon vanilla

Blend all ingredients for the filling in a blender until smooth. Pour into piecrust. Bake for 20 minutes. Let cool for 15 minutes. Raise oven to 425°F.

Topping
8 ounces sour cream
1 tablespoon vanilla
2 tablespoons sugar

Mix all ingredients together and smooth over cooked cheesecake. Bake again for 10 minutes. Cool before putting it in the refrigerator.

Chocolate Pecan Pie

The first time I tried to make this was a few years ago. It was Christmas time, and we were preparing the menu. For dessert, someone suggested pecan pie and chocolate pie. Then someone said that a chocolate pecan pie sounded good. So, I took it upon myself to come up with a recipe. Everyone enjoyed it and I know you will, too.

3 cups sugar
Pinch salt

7 tablespoons unsweetened cocoa
4 large eggs
1 tablespoon vanilla
1 (12-ounce) can evaporated milk
1 stick butter, melted
1 cup pecan halves
2 unbaked deep dish pie shells

Preheat oven to 350°F. In a medium bowl, mix the sugar, salt and cocoa together. In a small bowl, whisk together the eggs, vanilla and milk. Stir liquid mixture into the dry ingredients. Add the melted butter; stir until well blended. Sprinkle pecan halves in the pie shell, about 1/2 cup per shell. Pour the filling over the pecans. Bake for 40-45 minutes.

Crème Brûlée

Crème brûlée is translated "burnt cream." The burnt aspect is the sugar that is caramelized on the top of the custard. I always enjoy making this dessert because it allows me to play with my kitchen torch. You can find them in cooking stores for around twenty dollars. You can also put them under the broiler for a minute if you do not have a torch. The contrast between the warm sugar shell and the smooth and creamy custard makes for a perfect dessert.

2 cups heavy cream
5 egg yolks
1/2 cup sugar
1 tablespoon vanilla extract
1/2 cup or more of light brown sugar

Preheat the oven to 275°F. Whisk the cream, egg yolks, sugar and vanilla together in a medium bowl. Mix it up until it gets creamy. Pour this mixture into 4 ramekins. Place the ramekins in a baking pan. Fill the baking pan with hot water, to the halfway point of the ramekins. Bake for 45 minutes to an hour. After 45 minutes, check every 10 minutes. They are done when a knife stuck in the center comes out clean. Remove the ramekins from the pan and allow to cool for 15 minutes. Refrigerate overnight. Before serving, sprinkle a thin layer of brown sugar. Make sure it is a thin layer; also make sure that the entire surface of the custard is covered. Caramelize the sugar with a torch or the broiler. Serve immediately.

Crêpes Alyson

Alyson is my godchild. My sweet little girl has grown up into a beautiful mother of three. I have a picture of her when she was young. She is wearing a top that has the Strawberry Shortcake doll on it. Now grownup, I thought that a fancier dessert with strawberries would be an appropriate homage.

1/2-pound cream cheese at room temperature
2 1/2 tablespoons sour cream
5 tablespoons sugar, divided
1 1/2 teaspoons vanilla
8 *Crêpes* (page 146)
1 1/2 teaspoon butter
2 1/2 cups fresh strawberries, cleaned and sliced
1/2 teaspoon apple juice
2 tablespoons cherry liqueur

In a medium mixing bowl, combine the cream cheese, sour cream, 2 tablespoons of the sugar, and vanilla. Beat the mixture until smooth. Place 3 tablespoons of the mixture on one end of the crêpe. Roll the crêpe, refrigerate while preparing the topping. Place the butter and the remaining sugar in a large saucepan. Oven medium heat, cook for several minutes, stirring until the sugar dissolves. Add the strawberries and apple juice. Over high heat, bring the mixture to a boil; reduce heat to medium and cook for 10-12 minutes or until the mixture thickens. Add the cherry liqueur and flame the mixture. To serve, place 2 crêpes on each plate and spoon about ¾ cup of the topping over the crêpes.

Fudge Brownie Pie

This was the most popular dessert at Cannon's restaurant. This warm dessert was topped with a scoop of ice cream. We would have customers come in just to eat dessert and order the brownie. My version of this dessert is perfect for any chocoholic's cravings.

Brownie

2 1/2 cups sugar
2 sticks + 2 tablespoons melted butter
5 eggs
1 1/4 teaspoons vanilla
1/2 cup + 2 tablespoons cocoa
1 1/4 cup flour
1/4 teaspoon salt
1 1/2 cups pecan halves

Preheat oven to 325°F. Grease 2 pie pans. In a large mixing bowl, place the sugar. Add the melted butter and blend with a wire whisk. Add eggs and continue to blend until smooth. Add the vanilla and cocoa; mix well. Measure out flour and salt together in a separate bowl and mix. Add the flour to the batter, mixing it in slowly. Fold in the pecans and pour into pie pans. Bake for 40 minutes.

Frosting
10 ounces powdered sugar
3 tablespoons cocoa
1 3/4 teaspoons salt
2 tablespoons butter, melted
1/4 cup hot coffee
1 cup pecan pieces

Put sugar in a medium bowl. Add the cocoa, salt and melted butter and blend. Add the coffee slowly, blending with a wire whisk. Frost cool pies and top with pecans. Warm in microwave for 30 seconds. Top with ice cream before serving.

Fudge Pie

This was my mothers' most requested recipe. Everyone who ate it wanted the recipe so they could make it for their family. One might think that this recipe and the last one are alike. The brownie is more like a cake. The fudge pie is denser. It is delicious warm or cold. Compare for yourself, and see which one you like better.

1 square unsweetened baking chocolate
1/2 cup margarine
1 cup sugar
2 eggs
1/2 cup flour
1 teaspoon vanilla

Preheat oven to 325°F. Grease a 9-inch pie pan. Melt chocolate in a double boiler. Cream margarine until soft. Gradually add the sugar and continue mixing until creamy. Add eggs, one at a time, beating hard after each addition. Stir in the melted chocolate. Mix in the flour and vanilla. Pour into pie pan and bake 30 minutes. To serve, cut into wedges and top with ice cream.

Lemon Ice Box Pie

This classic southern dish is perfect for New Orleans hot summers. Not only is it served cool; it is very refreshing. But do not wait till summer to serve this. It is great for any occasion.

Crust
1 cup graham cracker crumbs
1 cup pecan pieces
1/3 cup sugar
1/3 cup butter, melted

Preheat oven to 325°F. Mix all ingredients together in a food processor. Press into a pie pan. Bake for 10 minutes and allow to cool before adding the filling

Filling
16 ounces cream cheese, softened
1 (14-ounce) can sweetened condensed milk
1/4 cup + 2 tablespoons lemon juice
1 teaspoon lemon zest

In a medium mixing bowl, beat cream cheese until fluffy. Add condensed milk, lemon juice and lemon zest. Mix until smooth. Pour mixture into crust. Refrigerate at least 2 hours before serving.

Peanut Butter Ice Box Pie

Everyone in my family likes peanut butter. There are some, you know who you are, who can eat peanut butter right out of the jar with a spoon. So, for all my siblings, this recipe is for you. Just remember, save some for everyone else.

12 ounces cream cheese, softened
1 (16-ounce) jar creamy peanut butter
1 1/4 cup sugar
1 1/2 tablespoon butter, melted
1 1/2 teaspoon vanilla
1 (8-ounce) tub whipped topping, divided
1 prepared chocolate graham cracker piecrust

In a large mixing bowl, combine cream cheese, peanut butter, sugar, butter, and vanilla. Beat until smooth. Fold in half of the whipped topping. Mound filling into piecrust and then smooth the top. Freeze for 10 minutes and then top with remaining topping. Chill at least 4 hours or freeze for at least 1 hour.

Pecan Pie

This is by far the most popular pie in the south. Pecan trees are abundant in the south from Georgia all the way to Arizona. I remember a trip when I was younger, picking pecans. You would have to shell them, one at a time, with a special pecan cracker. These days, it is easier to pick up a bag of pecan pieces to use in recipes.

1 cup light corn syrup
3 eggs
1 cup sugar

2 tablespoons butter, melted
1 teaspoon vanilla
1 1/2 cups pecan halves
1, 9-inch-deep dish frozen piecrust

Preheat oven to 350°F. In a medium bowl, mix the corn syrup, eggs, sugar, butter, and vanilla using a wooden spoon. Stir in the pecans. Pour into the piecrust. Bake on center rack of oven for 60-70 minutes. (Pie is done when the center is 200°F.) Cool for 2 hours before serving.

Sour Cream Cake

Another one of my mother's desserts, it is one that I do not remember eating. My older siblings told me that this was the dessert everyone wanted before she found the fudge pie recipe. A friend of my mother's made this cake for us after she passed away. This gave me my last recipe connection to my mom. I wish she could have made it for me.

1/2 cup butter
2 cups sugar
2 tablespoons cocoa
2 eggs
1/2 cup sour cream
2 cups flour
1 cup boiling water
1 1/2 teaspoon baking soda
1 teaspoon vanilla

Grease and flour a cake pan. Preheat oven to 350°F. Cream the butter and sugar. Add the cocoa and mix well. Add unbeaten eggs and blend. Add the sour cream, then the flour gradually. In a small bowl, pour water over the baking soda and add to the above mixture; mix well. Add the vanilla extract and blend in. Pour into prepared pan and bake for 30-35 minutes.

Sweet Potato Pie

The popular sweet potato shines when made into a pie. This southern classic is very popular. There are a few companies in New Orleans whose reputations are built on the sweet potato pie. The most commonly-used sweet potato is canned by Bruce Foods, out of New Iberia, Louisiana. Every year Bruce Foods, in conjunction with *Louisiana Cookin'* magazine, has a sweet potato recipe contest.

3 tablespoons flour
1 2/3 cup sugar

1 cup sweet potatoes, mashed
2 eggs
1/4 cup light corn syrup
1/4 teaspoon nutmeg
Pinch salt
1/2 cup butter
3/4 cup evaporated milk
1 unbaked 9-inch pie shell

Preheat oven to 350°F. In a large mixing bowl, combine the flour and sugar. Add potatoes, eggs, corn syrup, nutmeg, salt, butter, and evaporated milk. Beat well. Pour into pie shell. Bake for 55-60 minutes.

Turtle

This cookie was originated at the now closed McKenzie's Bakeries of New Orleans. The main reason for the inclusion of this recipe is my nickname. For some reason, I was given the nickname "Turtle" by some friends. They never explained the reason to me. My guess was I ran like a turtle playing softball. Maybe one day, I will find out the real reason.

Cookies
1/2 cup butter
1/2 cup packed brown sugar
1 whole egg
1 egg, separated
1/4 teaspoon vanilla
1/8 teaspoon maple flavor extract
1 1/2 cups flour, sifted
1/4 teaspoon baking soda
1/4 teaspoon salt
60 pecan halves

Preheat oven to 350°F. Lightly grease a cookie sheet. Cream the butter with the sugar until light and fluffy. Beat in egg, egg yolk, vanilla, and maple flavoring. Set aside. Sift together flour, salt and baking soda. Add dry ingredients gradually to the creamed mixture until you have smooth dough and then chill 2 hours. Shape the chilled dough into ovals like a turtle's shell. Dip bottoms into egg white. Press pecan halves into bottom to form a head and feet for the turtle. Place on cookie sheet. Bake for 10-12 minutes or until set. Allow to cool before frosting them.

Frosting
2 squares unsweetened chocolate
1/4 cup milk

1 tablespoon butter
1 cup sifted powdered sugar

In a small saucepan over medium-low heat, melt the chocolate and butter in the milk, and let stand until lukewarm. Mix in powdered sugar until it reaches the consistency to spread. It should be thick enough to "stand up" after being pushed through a decorating tube. If not thick enough, let cool or stand to thicken. Decorate top of cookie with frosting in a pastry bag. It should look like a chocolate kiss on top of the cookie.

White Chocolate Bread Pudding

Bread pudding is very popular in New Orleans restaurants. White chocolate bread pudding was first seen at Palace Café on Canal Street in New Orleans. My version is based on theirs. The main difference is the bread. Most bread puddings are made with day old French bread. I wanted something flakier; in this recipe, I use croissants.

3 cups heavy cream
10 ounces white chocolate chips
1 cup milk
1/2 cup sugar
2 eggs
8 egg yolks
6 large croissants
White Chocolate Sauce (page 111)

Preheat oven to 275°F. In a medium saucepan over medium heat, heat the cream but do not boil. Remove from heat, add the white chocolate, and stir until melted and smooth. In a double boiler over barely simmering water, beat the milk, sugar, eggs, and egg yolks together, and heat until warm. Blend the egg mixture into the chocolate mixture. Place the croissants into a 9x13-inch baking dish. Pour 1/2 of the chocolate mixture over the croissants. Let sit for 30 minutes, and then pour in the rest of the chocolate mixture. Cover with foil and bake for 1 hour. Remove the foil and bake for 15 minutes or until golden brown. Top with white chocolate sauce.

White Chocolate Mousse

This dessert is one I like to fix for special occasions. Every Valentine's Day, you will find it on my menu. It has a fancy name, but is very easy to make. The key is to make sure that the chocolate has completely melted. You can also use this recipe for chocolate mousse, substituting milk or dark chocolate for white chocolate.

8 ounces white chocolate, chopped into very small pieces, or white chocolate chips
2 egg yolks
2 tablespoons sugar
1/4 cup heavy cream
1 cup heavy cream
Chocolate sprinkles

In a large glass bowl, place the chopped white chocolate and set aside. Add the egg yolks and sugar to a small bowl and whisk until pale in color. In a saucepan, over low heat, bring 1/4 cup of the cream to a simmer, and slowly add the cream into the yolk and sugar mixture to temper. Pour the creamy mixture back into pan; stir with a wooden spoon until it coats the back of it. Pour hot mix through a strainer over the bowl with the white chocolate. Stir until completely smooth. In another bowl, whip 1 cup of the cream to almost stiff peaks. Fold half the whipped cream into the white chocolate mix to lighten and then fold in the remaining whipped cream. Spoon the white chocolate mousse into 4 serving cups and refrigerate until set, approximately 1 hour. Top with chocolate sprinkles.

Brunch

New Orleans is known for having fancy brunches. Commander's Palace, in the Garden district of New Orleans, invented the jazz brunch. Everyone should experience breakfast at Brennan's, in the French Quarter, at least once in their lives. The main focus of these brunches are the poached egg dishes. All of the dishes included here also make a great evening meal. My wife and I occasionally enjoy breakfast for dinner.

How to Poach Eggs
Calas
Crawfish Omelet
Eggs Benedict
Eggs Pontchartrain
Eggs Sardou
Grillades and Grits
Oysters Benedict
Pain Perdou

How to Poach Eggs

I have been keeping my recipes in alphabetical order. Poached eggs, however, are used in three of the recipes. So, here is how you poach eggs.

Get a medium or large pan. You want to make sure it is 4-5 inches deep. Put in enough water to have 3 inches in the pan. Add a pinch of salt and 1 teaspoon white vinegar. Bring the water to a boil. Reduce the heat of the water so it is right on the edge of not boiling anymore. Crack your egg into a small cup or bowl. This way, you don't use any broken egg yolks. Ease the egg from the cup into the water. Cook them 2 1/2 to 3 minutes. Remove them with a slotted spoon and let them drain. Put the egg on paper towels and gently pat them dry.

Calas

Calas are rice cakes or beignets. Louisiana is one of the largest producers of rice in the country. Calas, like beignets, are also a great dessert. If you are looking for something different, try calas. They are delicious; however, they take some preparation. It is best that they are started the night before.

3/4 cup warm water
2 tablespoons sugar
1 package dry active yeast
1 cup cooked white rice
3 eggs, beaten
1/8 teaspoon salt
1/2 teaspoon vanilla
1/2 teaspoon nutmeg
1 1/2 cups flour
1/2 cup powdered sugar, for serving
Steen's Cane Syrup, for serving

In a medium glass bowl, put the water, sugar and yeast. Allow to stand until the foam sets. Add the rice to the water; stir to combine. Cover the bowl with plastic wrap and allow to proof at room temperature 8 hours overnight. The next morning, stir the rice and mash it against the sides of the bowl with the back of a spoon. You want to create a contrast in texture, with some grains remaining whole and some crushed. Add the eggs, salt, vanilla, nutmeg, and flour to the bowl and stir with a spoon to combine. Cover the bowl again and allow to proof in a warm place. Preheat a deep fryer to 360°F. Use a large spoon to drop 2-tablespoon size scoops in the fryer. Do not overcrowd. Cook until golden brown, about 2 minutes, and then turn to cook on the other side for about 1 1/2 minutes. Drain the calas on paper towels. To serve, sprinkle with powdered sugar and drizzle with cane syrup.

Crawfish Omelet

This is a great morning dish after a crawfish boil. Omelets are the greatest vessels for leftover meats. You can put almost anything in an omelet. So, why not use leftover crawfish? You can also use any leftover vegetables from the boil. Whatever you use, it will be a great omelet.

8 eggs
1 tablespoon butter
1 pound crawfish tails
1/4 cup green bell pepper, chopped
1/4 cup onion, chopped
8 ounces mushrooms, cooked and sliced
8 slices cheddar cheese
Creole Seasoning Blend, to taste (page 146)
Mozzarella cheese, grated for topping

For each omelet

Scramble 2 eggs. In a small sauté pan over medium heat, melt butter. Sauté crawfish, bell pepper and onion, until onion is translucent. Heat a non-stick omelet pan over medium heat. Pour scrambled eggs into pan and season with Creole seasoning. Flip eggs gently in the pan. Add the crawfish mixture on half of the omelet. Add 2 slices of cheese and fold the omelet in half. Remove from pan and sprinkle mozzarella cheese on top. Repeat until all omelets are done.

Eggs Benedict

This is the most popular of all fancy egg dishes. Of course, there are conflicting reports of the creation of this dish. There are three restaurants claiming that the dish was created for a customer named Benedict. While New Orleans is not credited with the creation of this dish, I'll bet New Orleans sells more eggs Benedict than any other city.

8 slices Canadian bacon
4 English muffins, split and toasted
2 tablespoons butter, softened
8 poached eggs
Hollandaise Sauce (Page 108)

In a medium skillet over medium-high heat, brown the bacon. Put aside. Butter the muffin halves with butter.

To Assemble

Place 2 slices of English muffin on serving plate. Place a slice of Canadian bacon on each muffin half. Place a poached egg on top of bacon. Top with Hollandaise sauce and serve immediately.

Eggs Pontchartrain

Lake Pontchartrain is located on the northern and eastern side of New Orleans. Most dishes named Pontchartrain usually involve crabmeat. In this one, we are using oysters. One may think that fried oysters are strange on a breakfast plate, but in New Orleans, there are no rules or restrictions on what is eaten and when.

4 English muffins, split toasted and buttered
1 pound bacon, fried crisp and broken in half
8 poached eggs
Hollandaise Sauce (page 108)
32 medium-sized fried oysters (See *Traditions* section for recipe)

To Assemble

Place 2 English muffin slices on a serving plate. Lay 3 half strips of bacon on each half. Place egg on each muffin half and top with hollandaise sauce. Top each half with 4 oysters and serve immediately.

Eggs Sardou

Created at Antoine's restaurant in the French Quarter, this dish was named for Victorien Sardou, a famous French dramatist of the 19th century, who was a guest in New Orleans when the dish was invented. Like most dishes, other restaurants copied it. Most brunch menus contain this dish.

6 tablespoons butter, divided
2 tablespoons flour
1/2 cup milk
1/2 cup heavy cream
1 1/2 pounds fresh spinach, finely chopped
Creole Seasoning Blend, to taste (page 146)
8 large fresh artichoke bottoms
8 poached eggs
Hollandaise Sauce (page 108)

In a large sauté pan over medium heat, melt 2 tablespoons butter. Stir in the flour and mix well. Cook for 1 minute. Whisk in the milk and cream slowly; bring the sauce to a boil. Reduce the heat to a simmer and cook until the sauce coats the back of a wooden spoon, about 3 minutes. Stir in the spinach and season with the Creole seasoning. Continue to simmer for 1 minute. Remove from heat and keep warm. In another sauté pan over medium heat, melt the remaining butter. Add the artichoke bottoms to the pan and sauté for 2 minutes. Season the artichokes with Creole seasoning. Cover the pan with a lid and remove from the heat.

To Assemble

Place 2 artichoke bottoms on a warm serving plate. Spoon the creamed spinach in the center of each artichoke bottom. Place a poached egg on top of each artichoke bottom. Top with Hollandaise sauce and serve immediately.

Grillades and Grits

This dish can be found on New Orleans menus for brunch and dinner. Grillades can be made with either veal or beef. It is not known when this dish was created; however, it is a New Orleans original.

2 pounds veal round or beef round, ½ inch thick
Creole Seasoning Blend (page 146)
Flour
3 tablespoon canola oil, separated
1 medium onion, thinly sliced
3 cloves garlic, minced
1 small green bell pepper, finely chopped
1 cup tomato, chopped
1 tablespoon fresh parsley, chopped
1/4 teaspoon fresh thyme, chopped
3 cups cooked grits

Cut the meat into 3-inch squares. Season with Creole seasoning, and then dredge in the flour and shake off the excess. In a heavy skillet over medium heat, heat 2 tablespoons of the oil. Brown the meat lightly and drain on paper towels. Make a roux in the skillet with 2 tablespoons flour and the remaining oil, browning until it is a rich dark color. Add all remaining ingredients, except grits, to the roux and simmer until the mixture thickens, about 15 minutes. Return the meat to the pan, cover the skillet and cook until tender, about 1 hour, stirring often. Serve with grits.

Oysters Benedict

In this variation of Eggs Benedict, fried oysters, instead of eggs, are placed on top of the English muffins. Visko's, a closed restaurant of the New Orleans west bank, had a dish like this. Their oysters Meaux was made with a sauce that had a touch of mustard in it. My recipe uses the traditional Hollandaise sauce. This is another brunch dish that is great at dinnertime.

8 sliced Canadian bacon
4 English muffins, split and buttered
32 medium fried oysters
Hollandaise Sauce (page 108)

In a medium skillet over medium-high heat, brown the bacon.

To Assemble

Place two halves of English muffin on a serving plate. Place a slice of Canadian bacon on each muffin half. Place 4 fried oysters on each muffin half. Top with Hollandaise sauce and serve immediately.

Pain Perdu

Pain Perdu is French for "lost bread." This is the New Orleans version of French toast. The French bread that is used is usually one day old or stale, and considered "lost" because it was no longer fresh. Along with bread pudding, this offers a way to use less-than-fresh bread.

8 slices stale French bread sliced on a bias (angled) about 1 1/2-inch thick
1 cup half and half
4 eggs, beaten well
1/4 cup sugar
2 teaspoons vanilla
Nutmeg and cinnamon to taste
4 tablespoons butter
4 tablespoons canola oil
2 teaspoons powdered sugar

In a large bowl, combine the half and half, eggs, sugar, vanilla, and nutmeg; mix thoroughly. Soak the slices of French bread in the custard mixture until they are thoroughly soaked. In a large heavy skillet over medium heat, melt the butter and then add the oil. When the butter-oil mixture is very hot, fry the soaked bread slices on both sides, until they are golden brown. Sprinkle powdered sugar on bread before serving.

Beverages

New Orleans is well known for its beverages. The Hurricane, Absinthe Frappe, Ramos Gin Fizz, and the Sazerac are just a few of New Orleans's own creations. While not an original drink, my brother Mike, my friend Mike, and I, perfected the Girl Scout Cookie. The Brandy Milk Punch is the perfect drink for breakfast.

Absinthe Frappe
Simple Syrup
Bloody Mary
Brandy Milk Punch
Girl Scout Cookie
Hurricane
Irish Coffee
Mint Julep
Ramos Gin Fizz
Sazerac

Absinthe Frappe

Absinthe is illegal in the United States. It is made from the wormwood plant, which was said to cause insanity and death. Instead, in New Orleans, they use Herbsaint or Pernod instead of absinthe.

1 1/2 ounces Herbsaint or Pernod
1/2-ounce *Simple Syrup* (page 139)

Place a highball glass in the freezer until very cold, at least 30 minutes. Fill the glass with cracked ice. Pour the herbsaint and simple syrup over the ice and stir vigorously with a long-handled spoon until the glass begins to frost, about 1 minute. Serve immediately.

Simple Syrup

2 cups sugar
2 cups boiling water

Place the sugar in a heatproof container. Add the boiling water and stir until dissolved. Let cool to room temperature. The cooled syrup will keep, refrigerated, in a jar or container for up to a month. This makes 2 cups.

Bloody Mary

1 1/2 ounces vodka
3 ounces tomato juice
1/4 teaspoon horseradish
1/2 teaspoon Worcestershire sauce
3 drops Tabasco
1 celery stalk or pickled green bean or pickled okra

Stir the first 5 ingredients together over ice. Garnish with celery, green bean, or okra.

Brandy Milk Punch

2 ounces brandy
1 ounce *Simple Syrup* (page 139)
1/2 teaspoon pure vanilla extract
1 1/2 ounces milk
Freshly grated nutmeg for garnish

Combine all ingredients in a cocktail shaker with ice and shake vigorously. Strain into an eight-ounce rocks glass filled with ice. Garnish with a light dusting of freshly grated nutmeg and serve immediately.

Girl Scout Cookie

No, this recipe does not belong in the recipe section. This drink tastes like a Thin Mint Girl Scout cookie. It is best made in a large quantity and shared with a large group, like your Mardi Gras float riders.

1 part vodka
1 part green Crème De Menthe
1 part clear Crème De Cacao
1/2 part Kahlua
2 parts Milk

Mix all together. Refrigerate any remaining mixture.

Hurricane

This drink was created at Pat O'Brien's in the French Quarter. In the 1940s, Pat O'Brien needed to create a new drink to help him get rid of all the less popular rum that the local distributors forced him to buy before he could get a few cases of more popular liquors such as scotch and whiskey. He poured the concoction into hurricane lamp-shaped glasses and gave it away to sailors. The drink caught on and is the most popular drink in New Orleans.

1 ounce white rum
1 ounce Myer's dark rum
1 ounce Bacardi 151 rum
3 ounces orange juice
3 ounces unsweetened pineapple juice
1/2 ounce grenadine syrup

Combine all ingredients. Mix well, either shaking or stirring. Pour over crushed ice and serve immediately.

Irish Coffee

1 1/2 ounces Irish whiskey
Hot coffee
Sugar to taste
Whipped cream

Into a tall coffee glass rimmed with sugar, pour the Irish whiskey. Fill to 1/2 inch of the top with coffee. Cover the surface to the brim of the cup with whipped cream.

Mint Julep

2 ounces of bourbon
1 ounce *Simple Syrup* (page 139)
4-5 fresh mint leaves

Place the simple syrup and mint leaves in a glass. Muddle well to release the oil and aroma of the mint. Add the bourbon. Fill with crushed ice and stir well until the glass becomes frosty.

To muddle is to combine ingredients, usually in the bottom of a mixing glass, by pressing them with a muddler before adding the majority of the liquid ingredients. A muddler is a long pestle shaped often shaped like a baseball bat that is commonly made of wood, but modern designs can be found in stainless steel or plastic with teeth on the bottom. One end of the muddler is large and rounded and is used to mash ingredients. The other end is skinnier and flat.

Ramos Gin Fizz

Henry C. Ramos invented the Ramos Gin Fizz in 1888 in New Orleans. This drink was so popular that Huey Long brought a bartender from the Roosevelt Hotel, in New Orleans, to the New Yorker Hotel, in New York City, to show the staff there how to make this drink, so he could have it whenever he was there. The Roosevelt Hotel group trademarked the drink name in 1935 and still make it today.

2 ounces half and half
1 1/2 ounces gin
1/2 ounce *Simple Syrup* (page 139)
2 teaspoons fresh lemon juice
1 large egg white
1 dash orange-flower water
1 drop pure vanilla extract

Combine all the ingredients in a cocktail shaker with ice and shake vigorously until frothy. Strain into a rock glass and serve immediately.

Sazerac

The Sazerac is a New Orleans variation of an old-fashioned cognac or whiskey cocktail, named for the Sazerac De Forge & Fils brand of cognac that was the original prime ingredient. It is sometimes referred to as the oldest known American cocktail, with origins in pre-civil war New Orleans. On June 23, 2008, the Sazerac was proclaimed the official cocktail of New Orleans.

1 sugar cube
1½ ounces rye whiskey
¼ ounce Herbsaint
3 dashes Peychaud's bitters
1 lemon peel

Pack one old-fashioned glass with ice. In a second old-fashioned glass, muddle the sugar cube and 3 dashes of Peychaud's Bitters. Add the rye whiskey to the sugar/bitters mixture. Empty the glass with the ice in it. Pour the Herbsaint into the glass and swirl to coat the sides of the glass. Discard any excess Herbsaint from the glass. The rye mixture is then poured into the Herbsaint coated glass and the glass is garnished with a lemon peel.

Lagniappe

Lagniappe means a little something extra. The recipes here do not fall into any other category. These recipes are part of other recipes in this book. In here, you will find what I like to call the "building blocks of flavor." Here are seasoning blends, marinades, batters, and, of course, how to make a roux. While you will not find any finished dishes in this section, you will find the beginnings of delicious meals.

Blackening Seasoning
Bourbon Glaze
Cajun Popcorn Batter
Chicken Batter
Chicken or Pork Marinade
Chicken Stock
Creole Seasoning Blend
Crêpe Batter
Egg Wash
Hawaiian Marinade
How to Make a Roux
Roasted Garlic
Seafood Breading
Seafood Seasoning Blend
Seafood Stock

Blackening Seasoning

3 tablespoons paprika
2 tablespoons salt
1 tablespoon granulated garlic
4 teaspoons black pepper
2 teaspoons white pepper
1 teaspoon cayenne pepper
1 teaspoon dried thyme
1 teaspoon Italian seasonings

Mix well and store in a jar with a tight lid. It will keep for a year.

Bourbon Glaze

This glaze is great on any meat or fish you can grill.

2 teaspoons *Roasted Garlic* (page 148)
2/3 cup water
1 cup pineapple juice
1/4 cup teriyaki sauce
1 tablespoon soy sauce
1 1/3 cup dark brown sugar
3 tablespoons lemon juice
3 tablespoons onions, minced
1 tablespoon bourbon
1 tablespoon crushed pineapple
1/4 teaspoon cayenne

In a medium saucepan over medium-high heat, combine the water, pineapple juice, teriyaki sauce, soy sauce, and brown sugar. Stir occasionally, until the mixture boils, and then reduce the heat until the mixture is just simmering. Whisk roasted garlic into the mixture. Add the remaining ingredients to the pan and stir. Let the mixture simmer for 40-50 minutes or until the glaze has reduced by 1/6 and is thick and syrupy. Make sure it does not boil over. Cover until ready to use.

Cajun Popcorn Batter

1/2 cup corn flour
1 teaspoon sugar
1 teaspoon salt

1/2 teaspoon granulated onion
1/2 teaspoon granulated garlic
1/2 teaspoon white pepper
1/2 teaspoon cayenne pepper
1/4 teaspoon thyme
1/8 teaspoon basil
1/8 teaspoon black pepper
2 eggs, well beaten
1 1/4 cups milk

Combine all dry ingredients and mix well. Add eggs and milk. Mix until a wet batter is formed.

Chicken Batter

8 eggs
1 quart buttermilk
2 tablespoons salt
2 tablespoons black pepper
2 tablespoons cumin

Beat eggs. Add the rest of the ingredients and mix well.

Chicken and Pork Chop Marinade

3 cups vegetable oil
1 1/2 quarts Chablis wine
1 tablespoon granulated garlic
3 cups onion, minced
2 tablespoons celery salt
2 tablespoons salt
2 tablespoons black pepper
1 tablespoon tarragon leaves
3 tablespoon rosemary
2 tablespoon thyme
1/4 cup garlic, chopped
1/4 cup paprika
1/4 cup *Creole Seasoning Blend* (page 146)

Mix oil, water, granulated garlic, onion, celery salt, salt and pepper thoroughly until smooth. Add the remaining ingredients and mix well. Cover meat with marinade. Marinate a minimum of 12 hours.

Chicken Stock

2 pounds leftover bones and skin from a chicken, cooked or raw
Water
2 stalks celery, cut into 4-inch pieces
1 large onion, quartered
2 carrots, cut into 4-inch pieces
1 bunch fresh parsley
1 teaspoon salt
1/4 teaspoon black peppercorns

In a large stockpot over medium-high heat, put the chicken bones with enough water to cover them. Add the other ingredients and bring to a boil. Immediately reduce the heat to bring the stock to barely a simmer. Simmer uncovered at least 4 hours, occasionally skimming off the foam that comes to the surface. Remove the bones and strain the stock.

Creole Seasoning Blend

4 tablespoons paprika
4 tablespoons granulated garlic
3 tablespoons salt
2 tablespoons black pepper
2 tablespoons granulated onion
2 tablespoons dried thyme
2 tablespoons dried basil
1 tablespoon cayenne
1 tablespoon dried oregano
1 tablespoon ground bay leaves
1 tablespoon white pepper

Combine all ingredients in a mixing bowl and blend until fully mixed. Store in an airtight container. It will hold for 3 months.

Crêpe Batter

1 3/4 cups flour
1 tablespoon sugar
2 cups milk
1 egg
1/3 cup canola oil
5 tablespoons butter, melted, plus extra for pan

Place the flour and sugar in a medium-mixing bowl. Slowly whisk in the milk, egg, oil, and butter. Heat a nonstick pan or crêpe pan over moderate heat. Pour 1/4 cup of the crêpe batter into the center of the hot pan and tilt it in all directions. The batter should coat the pan in a light covering. After about 30 seconds, the bottom side of the crêpe should be lightly browned and the crêpe should be ready to be flipped. Shake the pan in order to release the crêpe, and then turn it by using a spatula. Cook the crêpe for an additional 15-20 seconds and then remove it from the pan.

Egg Wash

Mix together 2 slightly beaten eggs with 1 cup milk.

Hawaiian Marinade

Great for steaks or chicken, the marinade adds a tropical touch to your dishes.

1 (46-ounce) can pineapple juice
2/3 cup apple cider vinegar
1 cup sugar
3/4 cup soy sauce
2 teaspoons granulated garlic
2 teaspoons ground ginger

Mix all ingredients. Marinate meat for at least 12 hours, turning every 2 hours.

How to Make a Roux

The starting point for many Creole and Cajun dishes is a roux. A roux will make or break your dish. Roux is more than just a thickener. It also adds flavor to your gumbos and other dishes. You must be very careful with the roux. If you start smelling a burnt smell, throw it out. Make sure you do not splash any roux on you. It will leave a bad burn.

Equal parts canola oil or butter and flour

Heat oil in a pan over moderate to low heat. Add flour and stir until smooth. Cook, stirring constantly, to the desired color. Roux should be glossy in appearance. White Roux should be barely colored, or chalky. Pale or blonde roux should be golden straw color, with a slightly nutty aroma. Brown or black roux should be deep brown, with a strong nutty aroma. Do not burn. Even if you slightly burn a roux and that you have gotten the burnt pieces out, throw it away. The burnt taste will be present in the finished dish. Add your seasonings (onions, garlic etc.) before you add your liquid. Make sure your liquid is room temperature or cool.

Roasted Garlic

1 head of garlic
1 1/2 tablespoons olive oil

Preheat oven to 325°F. Cut about 1/2 inch of the top of the garlic head. Cut the roots so that the garlic will sit flat. Remove most of the skin from the garlic, but leave enough so that the cloves stay together. Place the garlic in a small baking pan, drizzle the olive oil over the top of the garlic and cover with foil. Bake for 1 hour. Allow the garlic to cool before handling it.

Seafood Breading

3 pounds corn flour
3 tablespoons salt
2 tablespoons black pepper
1 tablespoon cayenne
1 tablespoon paprika
2 teaspoons Old Bay Seasoning
1 tablespoon granulated garlic

Mix well. Store in an airtight container. It will keep for 3 months.

Seafood Seasoning Blend

2 tablespoons paprika
2 tablespoons granulated garlic
2 tablespoons ground bay leaves
1 tablespoon salt
1 tablespoon black pepper
1 tablespoon granulated onion
1 tablespoon thyme
1 tablespoon basil
1 teaspoon cayenne
1 teaspoon white pepper
1 teaspoon oregano

Combine all ingredients in a mixing bowl and blend until fully mixed. Store in an airtight container. It will hold for 3 months.

Seafood Stock

1 pound of shrimp, crawfish or crab shells or a combination
5 quarts water
4 carrots, sliced
4 onions, quartered
1/2 bunch celery, sliced
2 bay leaves
3 cloves garlic, sliced
2 sprigs fresh parsley
5 whole cloves
1 teaspoon black peppercorns
1 tablespoon dried basil
2 teaspoons dried thyme

In an 8-quart stockpot, combine all ingredients and bring slowly to a boil. Reduce heat, and cook 5-7 hours, occasionally skimming off the foam that comes to the surface. Replace water, as needed, 2 or 3 times. Remove the stock from heat, and strain. Press all the liquid from the shells and vegetables, and then discard them. Return stock to heat, and reduce to 2-3 quarts.

Index

1000 Island Dressing, 7, 58, 63
Absinthe Frappe, 11, 138, 139
Alfredo Sauce, 9, 99, 106, 107
Alligator Sauce Picante, 7, 68
Artichoke Squares, 5, 29, 30
Asparagus Soup, 6, 48
Bananas Foster, 5, 17, 18, 122
BBQ Shrimp, 7, 67, 68, 69
BBQ Shrimp & Grits, 67, 69
Béarnaise Sauce, 9, 90, 106, 107
Beignets, 5, 17, 18, 29, 34
Blackened Redfish, 5, 17, 19
Blackening Seasoning, 11, 19, 70, 77, 143, 144
Bleu Cheese Dressing, 7, 58, 64
Bloody Mary, 11, 138, 139
Boiled Crawfish, 5, 17, 20
Boudin Stuffed Pork Chops, 8, 82, 83
Bourbon Glaze, 11, 83, 143, 144
Brabant Potatoes, 10, 86, 112, 113
Brandy Milk Punch, 11, 138, 139
Brie en Croûte, 5, 29, 30
Broccoli & Cheese Soup, 6, 48
Bronzed Grouper, 7, 67, 70
Bruccoloni, 8, 82, 83
Bruno's Cajun Meatloaf, 8, 82, 84
Caesar Dressing, 7, 58, 59, 60, 64
Caesar Salad, 7, 58, 59
Cajun Boiled Potatoes, 10, 112, 113
Cajun Fried Pickles, 5, 29, 31

Cajun Fried Turkey, 8, 82, 84
Cajun Hot Wings, 5, 29, 31
Cajun Popcorn Batter, 11, 59, 143, 144
Cajun Popcorn Salad, 7, 58, 59
Calas, 11, 132, 133
Carrots with Orange Glaze, 10, 113
Catfish Étienne, 7, 70
Catfish with Pecans, 7, 67, 70
Charbroiled Oysters, 5, 29, 32
Cheesecake, 10, 122, 123
Chicken & Mushroom Soup, 6, 49
Chicken and Pork Chop Marinade, 11, 145
Chicken and Sausage Gumbo, 6, 47, 49
Chicken Batter, 11, 35, 37, 143, 145
Chicken Bonne Femme, 8, 82, 85
Chicken Cacciatore, 8, 82, 86
Chicken Clemenceau, 8, 82, 86
Chicken Delight, 8, 82, 87
Chicken Florentine, 8, 82, 87
Chicken Grande, 8, 82, 88, 89
Chicken Marsala, 8, 82, 89
Chicken Oregano, 8, 82, 89
Chicken Pesto Pasta, 9, 98, 99
Chicken Pontalba, 8, 90
Chicken Stock, 11, 22, 26, 44, 48, 49, 50, 53, 55, 56, 68, 73, 88, 89, 92, 96, 114, 117, 119, 143, 146
Chocolate Pecan Pie, 10, 122, 123
Cinnamon Pecan Apples, 10, 112, 114
Crab Bisque, 6, 47, 50

Crab Cakes, 7, 67, 71
Crabmeat Alfredeaux, 9, 98, 99
Crabmeat au Gratin, 7, 67, 72
Crabmeat Ravigote, 5, 29, 32
Crabmeat St. Francis, 5, 29, 33
Crawfish Beignets, 34
Crawfish Bisque, 6, 47, 51
Crawfish Bread, 5, 29, 34
Crawfish Étouffée, 7, 67, 72
Crawfish Fettuccini, 9, 98, 100
Crawfish Omelet, 11, 134
Crawfish Pie, 7, 67, 73
Cream of Crawfish Sauce, 9, 106, 107
Crème Brûlée, 10, 122, 124
Creole Catfish, 7, 67, 74
Creole Onion Soup, 6, 47, 51
Creole Seasoning Blend, 11, 22, 24, 31, 34, 35, 37, 38, 39, 43, 45, 48, 49, 51, 52, 54, 56, 57, 62, 69, 73, 78, 79, 80, 83, 84, 85, 86, 87, 88, 89, 90, 91, 92, 93, 94, 95, 96, 99, 102, 107, 110, 114, 115, 116, 119, 120, 121, 134, 135, 136, 143, 145, 146
Crêpe Batter, 12, 42, 143, 146
Crêpes Alyson, 10, 122, 124
Dirty Rice, 10, 112, 114
Egg Wash, 12, 21, 31, 36, 37, 41, 60, 70, 71, 74, 75, 81, 87, 143, 147
Eggs Benedict, 11, 132, 134, 137
Eggs Pontchartrain, 11, 132, 135
Eggs Sardou, 11, 132, 135
Fried Artichoke Hearts, 5, 29, 35
Fried Boudin Balls, 5, 29, 35
Fried Chicken, 8, 82, 90, 103
Fried Crab Claws, 5, 29, 36
Fried Crawfish Tails, 6, 29, 36
Fried Eggplant Sticks, 6, 29, 37
Fried Okra, 10, 112, 115
Fried Onion Rings, 10, 112, 115

Fried Oyster Caesar Salad, 59
Fried Parsley, 10, 112, 116
Fried Seafood Po'boys, 5, 21
Fried Soft-Shell Crab with Crabmeat, 7, 74
Frog Legs Abigail, 7, 67, 75
Fudge Brownie Pie, 10, 122, 125
Fudge Pie, 10, 122, 126
Garlic Mashed Potatoes, 10, 112, 116
Girl Scout Cookie, 11, 138, 140
Godchaux Salad, 7, 58, 60
Grillades and Grits, 11, 132, 136
Gumbo Z'Herbs, 6, 47, 52
Hash Brown Potato Casserole, 10, 112, 116
Hawaiian Marinade, 12, 143, 147
Herbed Rice Pilaf, 10, 117
Hickory Sauce, 9, 106, 108
Hollandaise Sauce, 9, 81, 88, 106, 108, 134, 135, 137
Honey Mustard Dressing, 7, 58, 59, 65
Hot Bacon Dressing, 7, 58, 63, 65
Hot Crab Dip, 6, 29, 37
Hot Crawfish Dip, 6, 29, 38
How to Make a Roux, 12, 143, 147
How to Poach Eggs, 11, 132, 133
Hurgy Lurgy, 10, 112, 117
Hurricane, 11, 15, 138, 140, 154
Hushpuppies, 10, 112, 118
Irish Coffee, 11, 138, 140
Italian Red Sauce, 9, 83, 95, 99, 101, 102, 106, 109
Jambalaya Cajun Style, 5, 21
King Cake, 5, 17, 22
Lasagna, 9, 98, 100
Leg of Lamb, 8, 82, 91
Lemon Ice Box Pie, 10, 122, 126
Lemon Sauce, 9, 106, 109
Linguini with White Clam Sauce, 9, 101
Maque Choux, 10, 112, 118

Marinated Crab Claws, 6, 29, 38
Meatballs and Spaghetti, 9, 98, 102
Meunière Sauce, 9, 41, 75, 77, 106, 109
Mint Julep, 11, 138, 141
Muffuletta, 5, 7, 17, 23, 58
Muffuletta Salad, 58, 60
Natchitoches Meat Pies, 6, 29, 39
New Orleans Bordelaise Sauce, 9, 110
Oriental Chicken Salad, 7, 58, 61
Osso Buco, 8, 82, 92
Oyster and Artichoke Soup, 6, 53
Oyster Dressing, 10, 112, 119
Oyster Soup, 6, 47, 54
Oysters Benedict, 11, 132, 137
Oysters Bienville, 6, 29, 40
Oysters Bordelaise, 9, 98, 102
Oysters Centola, 6, 29, 41
Oysters en Brochette, 6, 29, 41
Oysters Rockefeller, 5, 6, 17, 24, 40, 54
Oysters Rockefeller Soup, 54
Pain Perdu, 11, 137
Panéed Veal, 8, 82, 93
Pasta Jambalaya, 9, 98, 103
Peanut Butter Ice Box Pie, 10, 122, 127
Pecan Pie, 10, 122, 127
Perry Street Pasta Salad, 7, 62
Pesto, 9, 98, 99, 106, 110
Pomme Soufflé, 6, 29, 42
Pork Chops and Artichoke, 8, 82, 93
Potato Soup, 6, 47, 55
Pralines, 5, 17, 25
Ramos Gin Fizz, 11, 138, 141
Red Bean Soup, 6, 47, 56
Red Beans & Rice, 5, 25
Redfish Courtbouillon, 8, 76
Redfish Francis, 8, 67, 76
Roasted Garlic, 9, 12, 106, 110, 143, 144, 148
Roasted Garlic Crawfish Sauce, 9, 106, 110
Salmon Croquettes, 8, 67, 77
Sautéed Mushrooms and Onions, 10, 112, 120
Sazerac, 11, 138, 141
Seafood Breading, 12, 21, 31, 36, 41, 60, 70, 71, 74, 75, 81, 143, 148
Seafood Crêpes, 6, 42
Seafood Gumbo, 5, 17, 26
Seafood Seasoning Blend, 12, 32, 34, 40, 68, 72, 73, 75, 79, 81, 100, 104, 105, 143, 148
Seafood Stock, 12, 27, 33, 50, 51, 56, 68, 73, 76, 80, 143, 149
Seafood Stuffed Mirliton, 8, 78
Shrimp and Corn Chowder, 6, 47, 56
Shrimp and Tasso Pasta, 9, 98, 103
Shrimp Creole, 8, 67, 74, 78
Shrimp Fra Diavolo, 9, 98, 104
Shrimp Pasta Lorraine, 9, 98, 104
Shrimp Rehoboth, 6, 29, 43
Shrimp Remoulade, 5, 17, 27
Shrimp Scampi, 9, 98, 105
Simple Syrup, 11, 138, 139, 141
Sour Cream Cake, 10, 122, 128
Spinach Dip, 6, 29, 43
Stuffed Artichokes, 6, 44
Stuffed Crab, 8, 67, 79, 81
Stuffed Eggplant Pirogue Peggy, 8, 67, 80
Stuffed Mushrooms, 6, 29, 45
Stuffed Shrimp, 8, 67, 81
Stuffed Trout, 8, 67, 81
Sweet Potato Casserole, 10, 112, 120
Sweet Potato Pie, 10, 122, 128
Thai Peanut Vinaigrette, 7, 58, 61, 65
Turkey Poulet, 8, 82, 94
Turtle, 10, 129
Uptown Salad, 7, 58, 62

Veal Andrew, 8, 82, 94
Veal Marie, 8, 82, 95
Veal Parmesan, 9, 14, 82, 95
Veal Piccata, 9, 82, 96
Veal Saltimbocca, 9, 82, 96
Vegetable Surprise, 10, 112, 121
Vinaigrette Dressing, 7, 65, 66

VooDoo Rolls, 6, 45
Warm Spinach Salad, 7, 58, 63
White Chocolate Bread Pudding, 11, 122, 130
White Chocolate Mousse, 11, 122, 130
White Chocolate Sauce, 9, 106, 111, 130
White Sauce (Béchamel), 9, 106, 111

About the Author

TOMMY CENTOLA

Tommy Centola, the Creole Cajun Chef, has been cooking since he was eight years old. His first solo attempt was baking chocolate chip cookies. Under the watchful eye of his mom Mona Centola, Tommy started to expand his culinary knowledge. While in high school, he took a job at the 5-star New Orleans restaurant, LeRuth's. He was able to watch the running of a professional kitchen and learned about fine dining, cooking and presentation from the talented Leruths.

Tommy spent the rest of his time working at various restaurants. He eventually switched over to the distributor side of the business. Here, he is able to help many restaurants with his experience.

In 2005, Hurricane Katrina changed his life. He and his wife, Peggy, moved from New Orleans to Searcy, Arkansas. That is when his writing began. He writes a weekly article for his hometown newspaper and has published two cookbooks. He publishes two recipes a week on his blog. He loves to cook every chance he gets and enjoys sharing his knowledge of food. If he can inspire one person to cook New Orleans style, his mission has been accomplished.

You Can't Take New Orleans Out of the Cook is edited and republished for the Living the Life ™ imprint of Ladero Press and his second with the firm. *Creole & Cajun Comfort Food* is his first cookbook with Ladero Press and is available now.

Photo Credit: Michelle Pugh